VERY
SMALL
SHOPS

LAURENCE KING

Published in 2009 by Laurence King Publishing Ltd
361–373 City Road
London EC1V 1LR
Tel: +44 (0)20 7841 6900
Fax: +44 (0)20 7841 6910
E-mail: enquiries@laurenceking.com
www.laurenceking.com

Design© Laurence King Publishing Ltd 2009
Text © John Stones 2009

This book was produced by Laurence King Publishing Ltd, London

A catalogue record for this book is available from the British Library

ISBN: 978 1 85669 625 8

Designed by www.hoopdesign.co.uk

Printed in China

VERY SMALL SHOPS

JOHN STONES

LAURENCE
KING
PUBLISHING

CONTENTS

SMALL

INTERVIEW
AB ROGERS

SMALLER

INTERVIEW
MASAMICHI KATAYAMA
OF WONDERWALL

INTRODUCTION

Some of the best things come in small packages. Very small packages in fact. From jewellery shops to toy shops, it's a message that retailers know well. And it is something that applies beyond the exquisitely packaged object to the environment of the shop itself. Pulling the visitor into its little world, the small shop offers an intimate environment and exquisite experience many miles away from the cavernous mall or imperious flagship.

As can be seen by the stores featured in this book, there is a certain democratization when it comes to small shops. The limited size allows a level playing field between global chain and small independent, leaving famous designers and international brands sometimes struggling to match the ingenuity of small independents designing the shop themselves. While it is inconceivable that you could design a large store without engaging professional designers or architects, when it comes to little shops it is a very different matter.

Sometimes smaller shops are designed by designers from other disciplines. For instance, Canadian fashion

previous page IMAGE FORMING PART OF A PROJECT BY SWEDISH PHOTOGRAPHER JENNY NORDQUIST DOCUMENTING KIOSKS IN JAPAN.

right INTERIOR OF THE ITALIAN HOMEWARES STORE, ALESSI, OFF NEW YORK'S MADISON AVENUE, DESIGNED BY HANI RASHID. A MERE 46.5 SQUARE METRES (500 SQUARE FEET), THE STORE IS SMALLER THAN THE EARLIER SOHO BRANCH, ALSO DESIGNED BY RASHID.

9 ALBEMARLE STREET'S DESIGN IS THE
SUM OF THE BRIC-A-BRAC CHOSEN BY
PAUL SMITH.

designer Natalie Purschwitz is able to display the same originality in her shop as in the garments she produces under the Hunt & Gather label (see pages 118–123), and the product designers behind German spectacle brand Mykita (see pages 196–201), are able to bring the same meticulous attention to detail apparent in their eye wear to bear on their shop.

In the case of Paul Smith's 9 Albemarle Street, it is the retailer's taste itself that becomes the design. The store is a modern, luxurious reinvention of a bric-a-brac shop, where what you buy is the taste of Paul Smith, who selected the various (second-hand) items for sale, and the design of the store is just the sum of these objects. Sometimes, as in the case of Portuguese shoe shop Sneakers Delight (see pages 176–181) – the labour of love of retailer Igor Ferreira – no designers in the formal or professional sense of the word have been involved at all.

But small shops have undeniably also been a great opportunity for important designers to strut their stuff. And getting famous architects and designers to work on

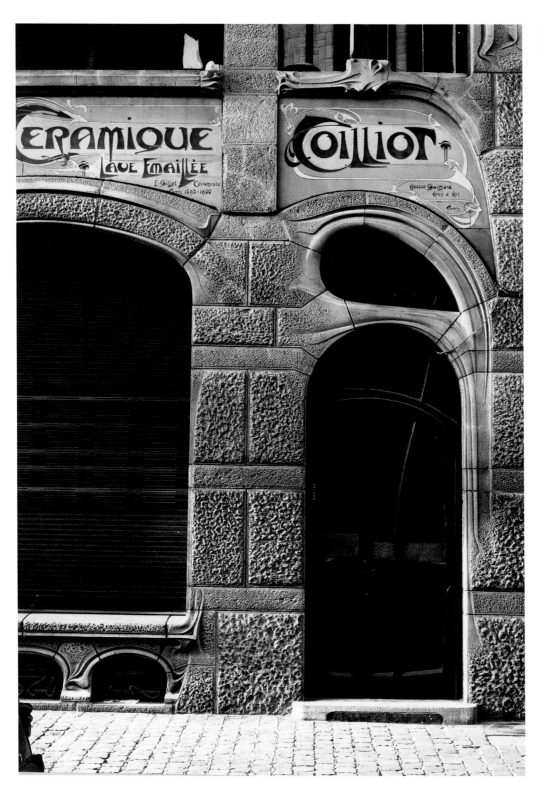

left ART NOUVEAU FAÇADE OF CERAMIQUE COILLIOT IN LILLE, DESIGNED BY HECTOR GUIMARD AROUND 1898.

shops is not as recent a development as might be thought – there is a tradition that stretches back to include shops such as the Viennese tailor Knize, designed by the great Austrian Modernist Adolf Loos, and the many beautiful Art Nouveau stores in France and Belgium, by architects such as Hector Guimard and others.

Unlike large stores, often the humblest kiosk or tiny grocery shop can become a visual delight in the hands of a skillful keeper. Of course, it is only relatively recently that shops haven't all been small. Over-restored medieval streets are now rather self-consciously home to so many small stores in Europe, their layouts constrained by the size of their ancient forebears. Sometimes, however, the pairing is felicitous, as in Shu, a shoe shop in Malta that transforms its historic shell into a Tardis (see pages 208–213). Kartell, the Italian company that specializes in contemporary plastic furniture, has many small shops dotted over the globe, but none as cute as the one in the medieval city of Caen in northern France. Tiny shops in places like Fez and Damascus preserve centuries of retail ingenuity, and often contrast favourably with their more modern counterparts.

Bridges such as the Ponte Vecchio in Florence (and the medieval, long gone, London Bridge) once housed a vibrant clustering of small shops. Perhaps their modern equivalents are airports, sprawling acres of small tax-free shops seeking to entice the traveller. The problem is that airports are dominated by small shops of such overwhelming slickness that they're hard to appreciate as such. More original solutions are thankfully evident elsewhere. Take, for instance, the conversion of Nissan's distinctive Cube cars into two stalls, one selling exhibition merchandise and the other snacks and drinks at 21_21 Design Sight, the design exhibition centre in Tokyo's Mid Town designed by Tadao Ando.

But kiosks and stands aren't really what this book is about. Arcades, a nineteenth-century innovation, come closer to prefiguring the kind of retail experience offered by many of the shops in this book. This is how Walter Benjamin, the influential early twentieth-century

cultural critic, described them in *The Arcades Project*, his unfinished magnum opus:

> The arcades are a centre of commerce in luxury items. In fitting them out, art enters the service of the merchant. Contemporaries never tire of admiring them, and for a long time they remain a drawing point for foreigners. An *Illustrated Guide to Paris* says: 'These arcades, a recent invention of industrial luxury, are glass-roofed, marble-panelled corridors extending through whole blocks of buildings, whose owners have joined together for such enterprises. Lining both sides of these corridors, which get their light from above, are the most elegant shops, so that the *passage* is a city, a world in miniature.'
>
> Walter Benjamin, *The Arcades Project*, page 3, translated by Howard Eiland and Kevin McLaughlin (Belknap Press of Harvard University Press, Cambridge, MA)

These arcades, so obsessively interrogated by Benjamin, are the precursors of both the modern luxury 'boutique', and its opposite, the shopping mall. When Benjamin was writing in the 1930s, these arcades were essentially a thing of the past, likewise the *flâneur* (or urban stroller and observer) that populated them. But some of the arcades have endured, such as the Galeries Saint-Hubert in Brussels and London's Burlington and Piccadilly Arcades. Lovingly restored, they continue to house small luxurious stores. The oversize, imposing Galleria Vittorio Emanuele in Milan, home to the original Prada store, continues to impress legions of visitors to the city.

It's perhaps not possible to write a book about small shops without briefly touching on the word 'boutique'. Is a small shop necessarily a boutique? To non-French speakers, it's a term that can conjure up different things to different people. Popular in the 1960s and 1970s, the word boutique implied exclusivity, flair, modest size and independence, but it now has a distinctly dated ring to it,

THE LA FUENTE LIQUOR STORE IN BARCELONA.

KARTELL'S DIMINUTIVE STORE IN THE MEDIEVAL FRENCH TOWN OF CAEN.

right TWO NISSAN CUBE CARS HAVE BEEN CONVERTED INTO MERCHANDISE AND FOOD STORES FOR THE ISSEY MIYAKE FOUNDATION'S 21_21 DESIGN SIGHT EXHIBITION CENTRE IN TOKYO.

below A TINY SHOP SELLING MUSICAL INSTRUMENTS IN THE MOROCCAN CITY OF FEZ.

though small shops, of course, have never gone away. The word boutique may have made a come back as generic term for the small and exclusive, whether for hotels or other exclusive enterprises such as investment banks, but when it comes to little shops outside the French-speaking world, it has generally fallen out of favour.

The word store (or shop) has a ring to an earlier, more robust kind of retail environment that many prefer. And the historical homes of many small shops, be they located in medieval streets or nineteenth-century arcades, frequently colours the design of the stores. If the large, brash chain store or flagship is usually contemporary in the way it is fitted out, the small store often adopts historic inflections in its design even if its concept is not an out and out retro one.

Few contemporary designs can compete head on with the handful of stores that have managed to survive with their century-old fittings intact. The conservative cultures of countries such as Austria mean that some of these retail environments are as they were centuries ago, such

as the Hofapotheke, a rococo pharmacy in Salzburg, or
the Imperial Bakery (k.u.k. Hofbäckerei) in Linz. But some
recent small store designs succeed in creatively engaging
with the experience of walking into those historic stores,
using traditional elements in a contemporary way, as in the
case of Ladurée in Monaco (see pages 226–231), or the
Peyton and Byrne bakery in London (see pages 240–243).

If an historical regression to earlier times is invoked by
many small stores, so too is a different kind of regression
– that to childhood. Speaking to the designers responsible
for the small shops in this book, there was one reference
that cropped up repeatedly – Lewis Carroll's surreal
children's tale *Alice in Wonderland* and its classic account
of massive differences in scales and sizes. While for
poor Alice, the experience is 'curiouser and curiouser',
for the shopper it is an experience usually intended to
be less disconcerting and more enchanting and playful.
It's more about the feeling of playing with a dollhouse,
the fascination of miniaturization, of a world that can be
grasped in its totality.

Naturally, the small shops that make up this book
come in different shapes and sizes. What counts as
small in some countries may be rather large in others.
For instance, the stores from the United States included
in this book are on the larger side, reflecting not only
the relatively recent urban fabric of the country but also
the cultural significance accorded to size. And it's not
something restricted to the United States – a Japanese
fashion company bristled at the idea of small shops. They
asked, why not look at their bigger, and by implication,
more prestigious shops?

In recent years, there has undoubtedly been a kind
of retail *campanilismo* to rival that of Italian warlords,
as luxury brands open ever bigger and flashier stores to
push rivals out of the limelight. Its epitome is probably
the stunning tower of glass that is Prada's Tokyo flagship.
Opened in 2003, its design by Herzog & de Meuron
wowed the world, though a handful of other spectacular
contenders could also be mentioned. While a few years
ago, these towers seemed the summit of cool, they now

opposite K.U.K. HOFBÄCKEREI, IMPERIAL BAKERY IN LINZ, AUSTRIA.

below left THE GIORGIO ARMANI TRAVEL RETAIL BEAUTY BOUTIQUE AT HONG KONG INTERNATIONAL AIRPORT, DESIGNED BY NUANCE-WATSON (HONG KONG).

below right QUINTESSENTIAL UNDERSTATEMENT – JOHN LOBB SHOE SHOP ON JERMYN STREET, LONDON. ITS TRADITIONAL CHARMS ARE AN INSPIRATION FOR JAPANESE DESIGNER MASAMICHI KATAYAMA (SEE PAGE 70).

also seem rather ostentatious, particularly in a different economic climate. Prestige is not always measured in size and there is always the danger of appearing parvenu. It is as well to remember that historically some of the most luxurious items have been very small and so has the environment in which they are sold.

For the more mainstream brands, the situation is somewhat different. Often the big brands hedge their bets, pursuing a marketing strategy with two prongs: in addition to the large supermarket-sized flagship, they will also maintain smaller stores, often in more fashionable areas, so as to get closer to the customer, in particular those they feel to be trendsetters. Smaller stores allow these brands to seem closer to the action and, crucially, less corporate and less like the global businesses they actually are.

The United States is, ironically, the location of one of the best small shop designs – Apple's Mini Store. Sadly, Apple was unwilling to supply information about these stores. Apple's main stores are often rather large and flashy, but in 2004 the Mini Stores were launched as complementary

smaller outlets, mainly located in malls (the modern arcades) to sell primarily 'on the go' products such as iPods and laptops. 'A big experience that fits in a small space' is how Apple described its Mini Stores at their launch, something that could well be said of many of the projects presented in this book. With walls and shop fronts laser-cut from steel imported from Japan, and seamless, totally uncluttered, white floors and ceilings, the Mini Stores share the same fastidious attention to detail as the iPods and computers on sale inside. Backlighting through plastic is another feature shared with the products themselves. The stores are a tour-de-force lesson in how to make a branded environment that is total in its commitment to the merchandise without being tacky or becoming a theme park. It's not clear why Apple is not pursuing this arm of its strategy with more enthusiasm, though the sheer cost of the design has been mooted as an issue.

The converse is true of most of the shops in this book. Their small size allows the designer freedom to pay attention to detail or use materials otherwise inconceivable (such as the Carrara marble for Azzedine Alaïa's shoe store, designed by Marc Newson (see pages 202–207). Or the small shop can be continually refitted, as in Lil Shop in Berlin (see pages 130–135) – the successor to the influential Commes des Garçons Guerrilla Stores – without it being ruinously expensive.

As is evident in the interviews with designers that open the three parts of this book, it's clear that what designers most enjoy when asked to design small shops is precisely this chance to tailor all the features to that particular environment, something usually prohibitively expensive for a large store.

The shops that follow are presented in descending size, in a telescoping effect that I hope mimics the experience in-store, encouraging the reader to gradually focus in on smaller and smaller objects. The book starts with small shops (between 100 and 150 square metres/1,076 and 1,615 square feet), then looks at even smaller stores before finishing with the tiniest stores under 50 square metres (538 square feet).

SMALL

INTERVIEW
AB ROGERS

Ab Rogers' London-based practice has been responsible for some of the most eye-catching small shops of recent years. Acclaimed designs for shops in London such as the opticians Michel Guillon (2003), the Miller Harris perfumery (2004) and the store for Russian fashion brand Emperor Moth (2006; see pages 88–93), as well as the Comme des Garçons flagship store in Paris that opened in 2001, show just how much innovation is still possible in retail design.

Why have you designed so many small shops – is it by accident or is it work that appeals to you? A bit of both I think. I am interested in doing very experiential shops, and it is easier to do that on a smaller scale. A smaller scale also makes it easier to convince a client to be more experimental. You can afford to create microsystems, and it is much harder to do that with larger premises. A small shop also means you can be quite extravagant with materials. But I must confess there was never any planning and we never set out to be retail specialists or to concentrate on small shops. If the brief was right, and we could do something exciting, we would do anything. And it's not necessarily about budget.

How important is drama in retail? I think it is extremely important. We very much see the product as hero, but we create experiential spaces to encourage engagement with the product. It is like a church. A church is a place to meditate in, or whatever. But over the centuries many churches have developed into incredibly lavish places, to help the process of engagement. What we are doing is similar. We want to create rich experiences that allow people to participate in a different way.

Which small shops do you particularly admire? Lunx [a Shiseido-backed perfumery in Paris] has sadly closed, but it was amazing – more of an environment than a shop. Griffin on Portobello Road [in London], designed by El Ultimo Grito, is also brilliant. And in New York, I really like Pop Burger and Pop Pizza, but I guess they aren't really shops.

right MICHEL GUILLON, AN OPTICIAN IN
THE KINGS ROAD, LONDON, FEATURES A
WALL PRESENTING GLASSES ON ACRYLIC
DRAWERS THAT ARE PROGRAMMED TO
MOVE IN AND OUT AT DIFFERENT SPEEDS.
THE SPACE IS MADE TO SEEM BIGGER
AND THE IMPACT OF THE KINETIC INSTAL-
LATION IS ENHANCED BY THE MIRROR
IN THE REAR OF THE STORE, WHICH
WAS DESIGNED BY AB ROGERS DESIGN
WITH SHONA KITCHEN, D.A. STUDIO AND
DOMINIC ROBSON IN 2003.

And your favourite shop? Herzog & de Meuron's Prada store in Tokyo – though, of course, that is not small.

Is there a cultural reason why some countries have such a strong tradition of designing beautiful small shops? I think it is a cost thing – in London or Tokyo often you just can't afford a large space. I think it's really as simple as that.

How is the working relationship different when working on a small shop? You are often dealing with one person. And a confident client gets better design. What destroys design is when you have to work for a corporate client and with a board of people. Working with one or two people you can create confidence. If it is a board you are dealing with then it all becomes very complicated. Everyone has an opinion. It is then no longer an intellectual process but a democratic one. And design can't be democratic.

What is important to keep in mind when designing a shop? I think it is important to have a narrative, to create something to work against. Here [at his practice] we create a narrative structure – this can be anything, a fairy tale for instance – and that sets out the criteria for us.

Is the use of mirrors in your designs there to make small shops seem bigger? Their use in the Emperor Moth store was more because I was interested in mirrors and the artist Robert Smithson's work at that stage than anything as specific as that. We have used mirrors in the past to make the space seem bigger, for instance in the rear wall of the Michel Guillon store. But with Emperor Moth it was more the idea of creating a mysterious place – a tardis, a space without boundaries.

left THE SUMPTUOUS INTERIOR OF MILLER HARRIS, A PERFUMERY IN LONDON'S MAYFAIR, DESIGNED BY AB ROGERS, SHONA KITCHEN AND D.A. STUDIO IN 2004.

26-31

SMALL

UBIQ
Philadelphia, Pennsylvania, USA
Rafael de Cárdenas, Architecture at Large
145m²/1,561ft²

It doesn't take more than a squint at this sneaker and menswear store to realize that its designer, Rafael de Cárdenas, is a big fan of Versace. 'Late 80s and early 90s Versace is pretty amazing,' he enthuses. 'I love the way it exports an Italian version of Vegas style.'

UBIQ was an unusually gratifying project for the designer as the budget was not very restricted. The brief was to create a high-end, aspirational outlet; something that would get some of the more exclusive brands on side for the client's other, more mass-market, stores. In short, the store was about leverage rather than instant profit, and so design was going to have to work hard.

Rather than rehearse the standard grunge, street aesthetic of sneaker stores, with its preponderance of concrete and steel, the design sought to hark back to an older language of luxury that would still draw in young, trend-conscious males. The shiny surfaces and busy, suggestive decoration of the Versace idiom gave Cárdenas a key to establishing a new vernacular for streetwear, and the store's location gave another.

UBIQ is located in an old nineteenth-century manor building that had undergone a standard, not particularly sympathetic, 'quasi-minimalist' renovation in the 1990s. But during the demolition process, Cárdenas uncovered a variety of features that he liked, including a large, magnificent fireplace and a highly decorative corniced ceiling in the rear of the space. The decision was taken to restore these elements and let them suggest the overall design of the store.

So the store was divided into two parts. The high-gloss area at the front, dominated by black and whites (and with a Versace-esque decorative graphic that is actually a camouflage pattern), presents the sneakers in the same way as glistening jewellery. A contrasting, comfortable, 'old school' area to the rear features warm woods and traditional detailing.

The front of the store, facing on to the street, was made deliberately brash, with bright lighting bouncing off the many reflective surfaces. The store is also about a metre (just over three feet) higher than the street outside. All

'IT'S AN EXPERIENCE INTENDED TO CREATE
A SENSE OF SELF-CONSCIOUSNESS AND
UNEASE IN THE CUSTOMER.'

MATERIALS
• White terrazzo floor
• Red oak flooring
• Chairs from eBay
• Black lacquered
  plywood cabinets
• Gold spray-painted
  electrical conduit
  boxes

of this adds to an experience that Cárdenas intended as creating a sense of self-consciousness and unease in the customer, as if they were on display themselves or were celebrities pursued by paparazzi.

While this element of display and forced theatricality becomes integral to the shop as a luxury experience, luxury is interpreted more traditionally as the customer reaches the rear of the store. There, in addition to the clothing display and fitting rooms, a more comforting experience awaits, combining a traditional Federalist look with the ambience of a Savile Row tailor, as red oak floor and mahogany joins the restored nineteenth-century plasterwork.

To the found elements, such as the restored original features, a large mirror discovered discarded in the storeroom and some chairs sourced from eBay, Cárdenas added wallpaper he himself designed. Appropriately enough, it is based on a peacock motif.

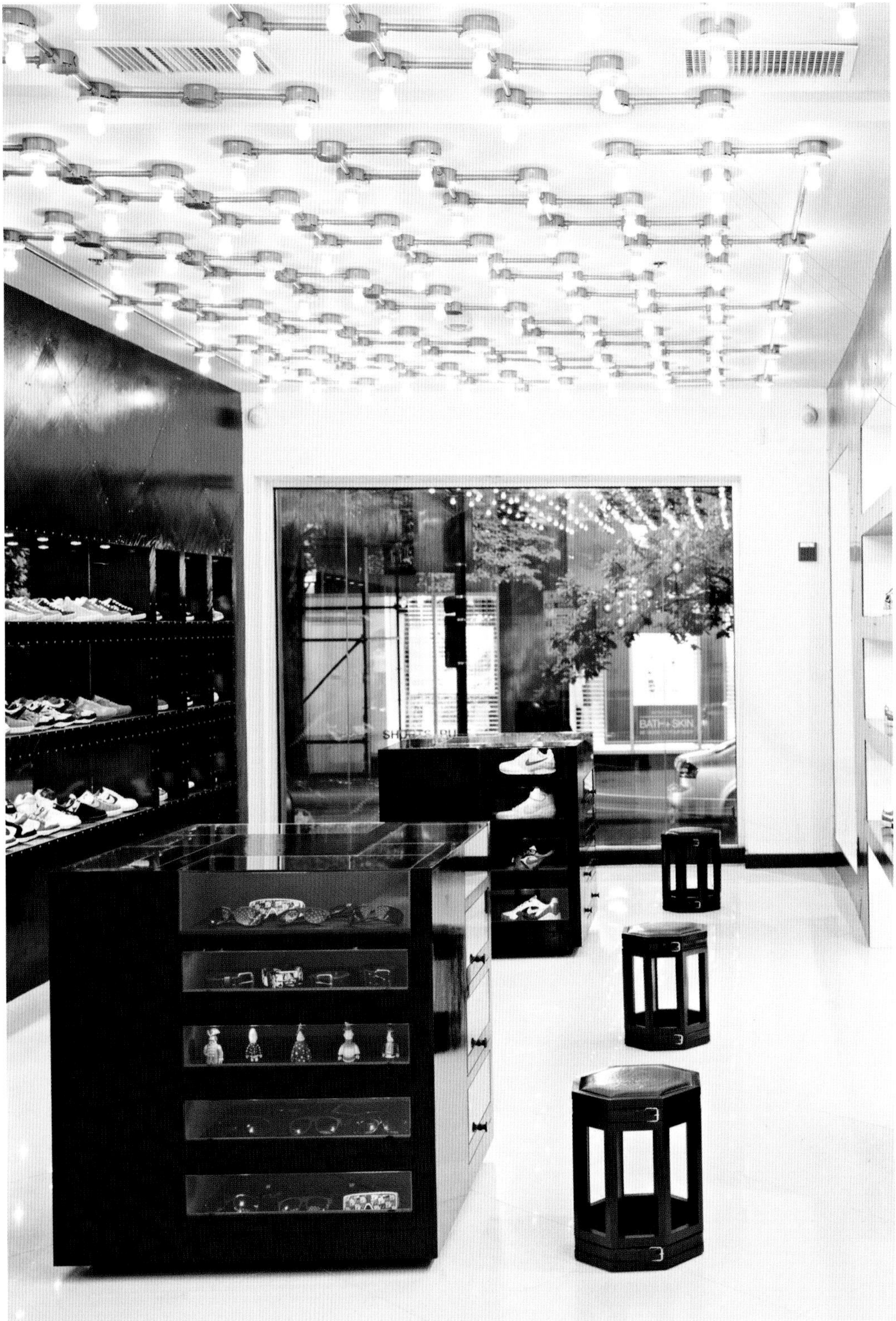

left VIEW THROUGH THE MAIN WINDOW OUT TO THE STREET.

right THE MAIN SHOP AREA HAS LIGHT BOUNCING OFF REFLECTIVE BLACK-AND-WHITE SURFACES, WITH THE MERCHANDISE SUPPLYING COLOUR.

A FALSE CEILING HANGS HEAVILY OVER THE CENTRE OF THE STORE, LEAVING ELEMENTS OF THE ACTUAL INDUSTRIAL CEILING ON SHOW FROM THE SIDES.

32-37
SMALL

SUNAO KUWAHARA
Tokyo, Japan
Steve Lidbury Design
141m²/1,518ft²

'The brief was very different. Often you get a thick file with information about the brand including its history, research and so on,' recalls Steve Lidbury, a British designer then based in Japan. 'But Sunao just brought some pieces of wood into the briefing and a couple of pictures showing concrete with a chandelier in front and he said to me, "This is the kind of atmosphere I am thinking about." And that was it, really.'

A protégé of Issey Miyake, Sunao Kuwahara is a high-profile designer of womenswear with a reputation for creating clothing that is both philosophical and architectural in its form. And this conceptual approach had to be reflected by Kuwahara's flagship store in Tokyo's B6 shopping centre, located in the city's fashionable Harajuku district.

'The clothes are very sculptural and textured. There are asymmetric cuts, a lot of volume to them,' says Lidbury. This, together with the materials presented to him by Kuwahara, encouraged him to create a gallery. 'Not your typical white box, but a retail gallery,' he quickly adds.

'WHEREVER YOU ARE IN THE STORE, YOU GET A NEW FRAGMENTED PERSPECTIVE.'

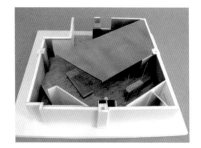

The design developed out of a juxtaposition of raw, heavily textured finishes suggested by the objects at the briefing, with contrasting glistening glass and mirror surfaces and a wish for the whole space to have a strong, sculptural quality. Cheap scaffolding wood was chosen for the floor because of its rough, unfinished quality. Sumi ink – the sooty ink traditionally used by Japanese artists – was mixed with mortar for the walls, giving them an intentional inconsistency and, therefore, depth. Contrasting reflective glass surfaces seem like pools of water in which the sparsely hung clothing is either floating or reflected.

The space was deliberately fragmented in Lidbury's design. 'There are different avenues,' he explains. 'Almost wherever you are in the store, you get a new fragmented perspective. At the entrance you don't see everything. You know there is something over there, so exploration is encouraged. As you walk around you can investigate a little.'

Dark and dramatic, a triangular dropped ceiling hovers above the store, seemingly balancing around the central column. The area directly beneath it is reserved for select merchandise, creating a subliminal subdivision in the store. 'It is not too heavy, it just feels a bit different,' says Lidbury. 'As soon as you step out of the space under it, the ceiling goes higher and the atmosphere feels different, so you understand the kind of segregation in the overall environment.'

Those higher areas are, in fact, the original ceiling, which was left in place together with all its ductwork and pipes. Painted white and strongly lit with fluorescent tubes, it gives an overall lightness without disturbing the store's moody, textured, atmospheric environment.

MATERIALS
• Scaffolding wood for flooring
• Sumi ink mixed with mortar for the walls
• Glass panelling, partly covered with a grey transparent film

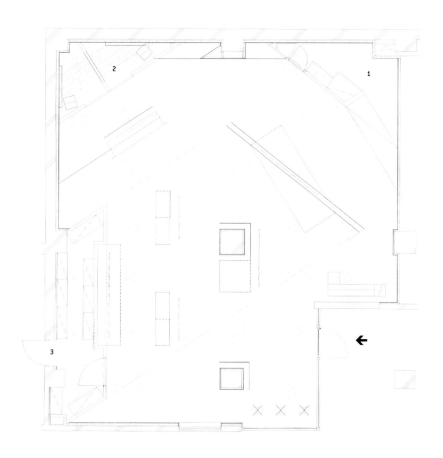

opposite top THE USE OF TRADITIONAL
SUMI INK MIXED WITH MORTAR CREATES
EERIE, UNEVENLY COLOURED WALLS.

above THE GLASS DISPLAYS HAVE AN
ETHEREAL PRESENCE IN THE STORE
AND CONTRAST WITH THE ROUGH
SCAFFOLDING WOOD USED FOR THE
FLOOR.

left and opposite bottom THE CLOTHES
ARE REFLECTED IN THE GLASS TABLES,
OR SEEM TO FLOAT ON THEM, AS IF ON
WATER.

F-SHOP HAMBURG

Hamburg, Germany
blauraum architekten/FREITAG Lab
140m²/1,507ft²

below THE STORE IS LOCATED ON AN INCLINED SITE CLOSE TO HAMBURG'S DOCKS.

opposite THE SHOP WITHIN A SHOP: A RECREATED SHIPPING CONTAINER IS PLACED ON STILTS UPON INTERIOR ASPHALT THAT MIMICS THE ROAD OUTSIDE.

'Given that we make bags out of recycled truck tarpaulins, we soon came up with the idea of using the truck container as part of the display,' says Marcus Freitag, who, together with his brother Daniel, founded the bag shop and brand of FREITAG. Both are graphic designers, and it's not surprising to hear that they were intimately involved in the design of their Hamburg flagship store, the first outside their native Switzerland. While they consider themselves all-round designers, they did, however, decide to bring in friends of theirs – Hamburg-based blauraum architekten – to design and execute the store.

The brothers had initially been attracted to Hamburg's slightly desolate harbour area for logistic reasons, but it also fitted nicely with the character of their product. The original Hamburg store was half its current size, but when the gallery next door became vacant they took that too and knocked down the separating wall.

They now had the space to do something more ambitious, and so decided to introduce a truck container – not just

'IT HAS THE FEELING OF THE SPACE OF A TRUCK. IT IS A BIT CLAUSTROPHOBIC BUT IT IS ALSO VERY SPECIAL.'

any one, but the very largest 12-metre (40-foot) size – and give the store something of the feeling of a truck stop. While they would have liked to have used a real container (as they did for their astonishing Zurich flagship, to tie in with their recycling ethos), removing and rebuilding the roof was impractical. So, adhering to the exact dimensions, and using wood panelling rather than metal, a container was recreated in situ. 'It has the feeling of the space of a truck. It is a bit claustrophobic but it is also very special,' says Marcus.

The container has mirrors on its exterior, which he says 'bring the traffic into the space'. The recreated container is positioned on support stilts above a floor that mimics the slope of the road outside. Unusually, asphalt is used for the interior floor covering.

This special container has room for 1,000 bags. As every one of them is unique, each is in its own box, which features a picture of that particular bag. A flexible rack system (common to all the company's stores) allows more product to be shown and stored than if the bags were on open display, explains Marcus.

Just as efficiency and logistics are essential aspects of both the original tarpaulins and FREITAG's reuse of them, these qualities are also integral to the Hamburg shop. It functions as the storage centre and hub where all the web orders are processed and dispatched – so, when the shop is empty, the staff are not left bored and staring at the passing traffic.

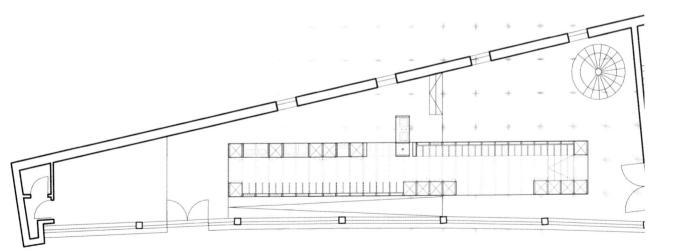

FREITAG'S DISPLAY SYSTEM ALLOWS THE PACKAGED BAGS, EACH WITH AN IMAGE OF THE UNIQUE PRODUCT INSIDE, TO PROVIDE A DECORATIVE ELEMENT IN THE OTHERWISE AUSTERE STORE.

MATERIALS
- Duripanel used for the recreated container
- Asphalt surfacing on the sloped floor inside the store
- Large mirrors to clad the exterior of the container

CONTRAPUNTO

Santiago, Chile
Lipthay + Cohn + Contenla
120m²/1,292ft²

THE BOOKSHOP SEEMS TO BE CARVED
OUT OF ITS IMPOSING TRAVERTINE
MARBLE FRONT.

The commission to design a new bookstore for
Contrapunto was both exciting and a bit daunting,
says Nicolas Lipthay. Daunting because Contrapunto
was not only the client, but also, as Chile's primary seller
of design and architecture books, somewhere where he
himself would often go to browse and shop. And it also
had a clientele especially finely tuned to design. 'It was
important to make good architecture – they sell design
themselves,' says Lipthay.

What the architects had to play with was an irregularly
shaped space, some 5 metres (16 feet) high and with
a 10-metre (33-foot) facade. So they decided on an
imposing angled façade that was to become the store's
principal feature, and covered it in a discrete but luxurious
open-pore travertine marble. This monumental block
is broken by a relatively shallow but long window that
showcases the books and pulls in passers-by through a
full-height entrance.

The volume of the shop window follows seamlessly
inside. There it becomes the main counter of the store,

housing the tills and other essentials and defining the area behind which the sales staff sit.

The façade conceals a second storey, dedicated to medical books, which is reached by an elegant internal staircase. Making this area abut the front of the store freed up the side and rear perimeter walls, which are given over to a giant 3.8-metre (12½-foot) bookcase on which the larger illustrated books are displayed and stored. At night, an enormous, louvred, black-painted iron door folds out from the neighbouring marble to secure the premises.

Rich lapacho wood from Bolivia was specified for the floor, and darker paquio wood, also from Bolivia, was used for the bespoke bookcases that envelop the space. Overall, the effect the architects aimed for was a neutral, timeless and classy environment that would be beautiful without upstaging the books, which naturally had to remain the stars of the show.

above THE CONTINUATION OF THE MARBLE SHOPFRONT SERVES AS THE MAIN COUNTER AREA FOR THE STORE.

left VIEW DOWN FROM THE FIRST FLOOR.

opposite FROM BOTTOM: GROUND- AND FIRST-FLOOR PLANS.

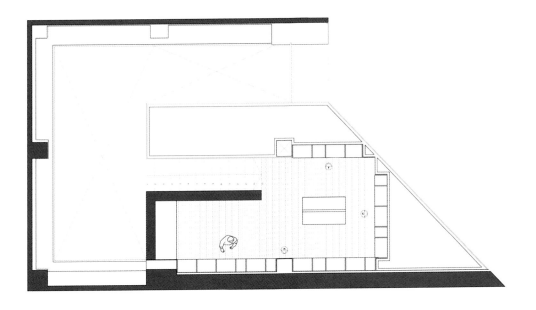

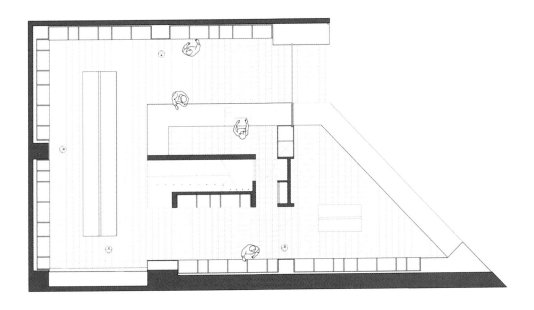

'IT WAS IMPORTANT TO MAKE GOOD ARCHITECTURE – THEY SELL DESIGN THEMSELVES.'

MATERIALS
- Open pore travertine marble and crystal for the façade
- Black iron for the entrance door
- Paquio wood for the book shelves
- Lapacho wood floors

50-53

SMALL

CONCEPTS

Cambridge, Massachusetts, USA
Soldier Design
112m²/1,206ft²

Concepts had started in 1996 as a 'snow, skate and culture' boutique; a shop within a shop in The Tannery, a long-established Boston retailer owned by Tarek Hassan. But in 2008, it was decided that the time was right for Concepts to have an identity of its own and to create a dedicated space where the retail experience could be further developed and controlled.

As many of its core customers were 'skaters or hipsters', and 'quite judgemental and in the know', the store needed to look good without seeming to be trying too hard, says Bobby Riley of Soldier Design. What he hoped to achieve was a deconstructed shop, something underpinned by the store's main visual effect – wood ribbing that goes right through the space, crossing from wall to ceiling.

The visual idea of layers of wood is a reference, none too subliminal, to the laminated wood used for the skateboards of Concept's original clientele. This visual theme of layers is mirrored in miniature in the apple plywood that makes up the ribs themselves.

'SHOPPERS FEEL THEY ARE AROUND A CAMPFIRE OR IN SOME KIND OF URBAN EQUIVALENT TO A LOG CABIN.'

opposite TWO ECOSMART FIRES ON THE CENTRAL COUNTER CREATE AN EFFECT SUGGESTIVE OF AN URBAN LOG CABIN.

left LAMINATE RIBBING, EVOCATIVE OF THE CONSTRUCTION OF SKATEBOARDS, ADORNS THE FULL LENGTH OF THE STORE.

THE FRESCOED CEILING, FEATURING
MEDICINAL HERBS, WAS PAINTED BY
MONICA TRENKLER.

THE WALLS AND FURNITURE SHARE
THE SAME SOFT ORGANIC WHITE FORM,
SET OFF BY THE COBBLED FLOOR AND
MERCHANDISE.

60-65
SMALL

JIN'S GLOBAL STANDARD NAGAREYAMA
Nagareyama-shi, Chiba, Japan
Ryuji Nakamura Architects
104m²/1,119ft²

A corner site in a large mall in the suburb of Nagareyama near Tokyo is an unlikely spot for retail theatre of the kind successfully envisaged by Ryuji Nakamura for opticians Jin's Global Standard. The shop is composed of a series of obliquely angled walls, less than a metre (just over three feet) apart. By offering a short cut across the corner site, these entice passers-by into the store.

Rather than setting up a disorienting *Alice in Wonderland* effect, Nakamura says the walls provide comfortable folds that are rather like a coral, creating a shopping experience akin to tropical fish grazing a reef. The walls also greatly increase the surface area available for display.

Despite the limited floor area, the walls also create an intimate, readable space in which potential purchasers can try on glasses in comfort and privacy, without feeling the undue pressure of shopping in a more open, conventionally exposed arena. The full height of these walls accentuates this element of privacy, but became a subject of discussion because the shop staff are not

MATERIALS
• Bespoke light fitting
• Readymade wall
  panelling

always able to see shoppers and potential shoplifters. However, it was decided that the benefits of this welcoming space outweighed the risk of theft, lessened in any case by the fact that only frames, rather than glasses complete with lenses, are on display.

The angled walls create corridors that are 'domesticated' by their treatment. They feature shallow wall shelving on which the spectacles themselves are carefully positioned in such a way as to give the overall impression of a wallpaper pattern. The bases of the walls are decorated with domestic looking off-the-shelf panelling and railing. Mirrors are hung on the walls as if they were framed paintings in a house, says Nakamura. Izumi Okayasu, in charge of the lighting design, chose to go for bespoke light fittings with exposed bulbs. These allow light to bounce off the white walls without any need for further lighting.

Two radial passages cut through these diagonal walls, drawing shoppers to the counter and staff if they are so inclined. The shop's inside perimeter walls are false, and it is behind them that the service elements are located: the

sales counter, an eye-testing facility, a waiting area, and a processing space.

As well as tempting in local shoppers, the design has gone on to win prizes around the world.

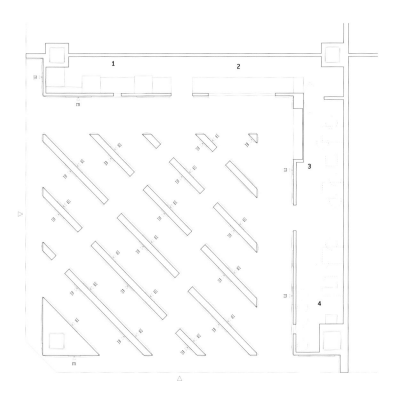

'THE WALLS PROVIDE COMFORTABLE
FOLDS RATHER LIKE A CORAL, CREATING
A SHOPPING EXPERIENCE AKIN TO TROPICAL
FISH GRAZING A REEF.'

SMALLER

INTERVIEW
MASAMICHI KATAYAMA

While the shops he designed for A Bathing Ape catapulted Masamichi Katayama and his appropriately named studio, Wonderwall, into the international limelight, his spectacular style has also been brought to bear on a series of smaller luxury boutiques, as well as restaurants and bars. Designs for Uniqlo stores around the world have ensured that not only those who can afford to visit the most expensive and exclusive of boutiques have had the chance to revel in his retail environments.

What are the differences in the way you approach the design of a small boutique compared with the design of a large store like Uniqlo? Is a small floor space a constraint or an opportunity? Whether it be a small boutique or a large boutique, my approach starts from the same place. Certainly there are constraints that may be particular with a smaller space, as it makes it a bit harder to create various different scenarios, but once the direction is determined the rest is the same as designing a larger space.

What is the most important consideration when it comes to designing a small shop? As I mentioned, it is very important to determine the overall direction and concept for each specific store or space. I try to focus on the message the brand is trying to convey. While I consider myself very devoted personally to each project, I design with the hope that the client's own dedication and passion toward the brand is exuded from the interior design.

How vital is an element of awe, surprise or wonder to your approach to retail design? I would say that it is more important for the consumer to experience the sense of discovery than to be surprised.

Which small shops, not designed by you, do you admire? There are many shops I admire, but I am often drawn to older establishments and speciality stores. There is this sense of comfort and assurance with a wide selection of merchandise. I also like stores where you feel the owner's sense of pride toward their products. For example, the John Lobb store in London has this certain insurmountable atmosphere, which I like regardless of the size or the design of the store.

Where do you go for inspiration when you are designing retail spaces – is it to other shops or to art, film etc? I get inspiration from various fields, such as history, architecture, art, books, films and so on. But not in a literal way – it's the sensibility or the spirit of these things that inspires me.

How do you develop the design of a shop from scratch – do you create a narrative, decide on a visual hook, or develop it out of the brand? Generally speaking, I tend to develop the interior designs out of the brand. Communicating with the client is very important to me. To understand their vision and expectations, and even how they want to grow the brand. I also study and review the products to be sold in the space to help me understand the brand and how the customer may react to it.

'Imagine the apartment of a mathematics professor who has good taste but is a bit weird.' That, says Alexander Plajer of Berlin-based Plajer & Franz Studio, was what they set out to create for this store, which sells clothes and accessories such as leather-covered helmets to Berlin's more fashion-conscious men.

Plajer had met the client at a party, where the latter mentioned plans to open a high-end male fashion store, but was struggling to come up with a concept that worked. When the briefing meeting was duly arranged, the client had little more than a name – Geometry – and it transpired that he was a big fan of mathematics and had indeed studied the subject at university. Plajer says they quickly decided against any overly literal interpretation of the store's name ('it is like making an airport in the shape of an aeroplane') and instead developed the 'nice but weird' space that you can see.

'We are really tired of the whole shabby chic thing,' says Plajer. 'Especially here in Berlin, we have had it for years. Leave the floors and walls and put in a chandelier

GEOMETRY
Berlin, Germany
Plajer & Franz Studio
100m²/1,076ft²

opposite THE SHOPFRONT OF GEOMETRY, GIVING A GLIMPSE OF THE SOMBRE AND ECCENTRIC INTERIOR.

right and far right THE WINDOW DISPLAY INCLUDES STRIPS OF GLASS STRATEGICALLY PLACED TO CREATE GEOMETRIC PATTERNS OUT OF THE REFLECTIONS OF WINDOW SHOPPERS.

'INCLUDING 1950s FURNITURE REINFORCES
THE IDEA OF THIS SPACE BEING THE WEIRD
PROFESSOR'S APARTMENT.'

MATERIALS
- 'Mikado' suspension lamp designed by Miguel Herranz for Luzifer
- Oiled oak flooring
- Bleached oak bespoke furniture
- Large photographs printed on matt paper

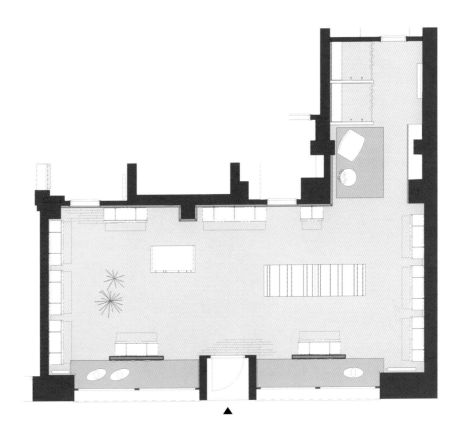

— it may be good marketing for Comme des Garçons, but it is so boring.' So, a warm greyish mud colour was chosen for the walls and the smoked oak floors were oiled to stop them from being too reflective — all aiming to create the feel of an apartment where the curtains remain drawn. For similar reasons, the extensive mirrors in the store are placed behind brown glass for a more muted effect.

To add an element of shock, specially commissioned photographs of animal skeletons (zebra, hippopotamus and warthog) take pride of place on the walls and in the changing rooms. These photographs have a matt surface, again to dampen reflections. The light fittings (made of painted veneered wood) echo the skeletons while being suggestive of a game of Mikado (or 'pick-up sticks'), while overhead spots are used for deliberately sharp highlighting. Bleached oak was specified for the shelving and counter, making their irregular joints visible and providing a contrast in texture and colour.

Including 1950s furniture reinforces the idea of this space being a 'professor's apartment'. As for geometry, the one place where this does become explicit is in the front window display. Here, cleverly angled mirrors have the effect of chopping window shoppers into interesting shapes.

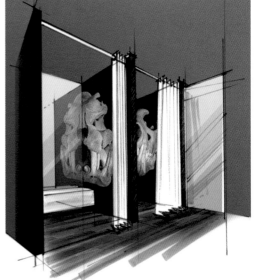

left SPECIALLY COMMISSIONED PHOTOGRAPHY OF UNUSUAL ANIMAL SKELETONS IS PLACED AROUND THE SHOP, AS HERE IN THE CHANGING ROOMS.

below SKETCH SHOWING THE SKELETAL DECORATION IN THE CHANGING ROOMS.

opposite 1950S FURNITURE IS SCATTERED ABOUT THE SPACE TO SUGGEST IT IS THE PERSONAL APARTMENT OF AN ECCENTRIC PROFESSOR.

opposite THE SIMPLE GLASS FRONTAGE OF UNION'S SECOND NEW YORK STORE LETS THE INTERIOR DO THE TALKING.

below FLOOR PLAN SHOWING HOW THE VARIOUS SECTIONS OF THE STORE ARE ARTICULATED BY THE DIFFERENT DIRECTIONS OF THE WOOD FLOORING.

Streetwear has become so firmly enmeshed in mainstream culture and global megabrands that it is easy to forget that it originally started off as a small counter-culture supported by equally small shops. One such shop was UNION, which opened in SoHo, New York, in 1989.

Nearly two decades later, the shop upped sticks from its original location on Spring Street, only to move a few doors down to slightly bigger premises. Initially conjoined with Supreme and Stüssy, it's now a stand-alone business, selling contemporary fashion to urban males with finely attuned noses to what is cool and what isn't. The store is proud of its pioneering status. Consequently its design, by Harry Allen & Associates, incorporates elements of the present in the previous incarnation, such as the wooden counter area (made from Yellow Pine sourced from southern states in the US), to maintain continuity and give a sense of familiarity.

Authenticity to its location, and Manhattan in particular, was also an important consideration, and this was

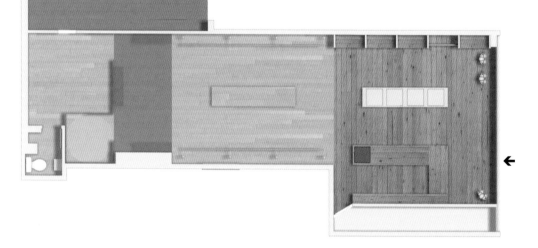

78-81

SMALLER

UNION NY
New York, New York, USA
Harry Allen & Associates
98m²/1,055ft²

'THE DEMO PROCESS IN NEW YORK IS SO INTERESTING THAT WE DECIDED TO PRESERVE IT.'

opposite THE COUNTER, MADE OF SOUTHERN YELLOW PINE, IS A MAIN FEATURE OF THE STORE AND A POINT OF CONTINUITY WITH UNION'S ORIGINAL NEW YORK STORE.

far left THE DUCTING AND EXPOSED RAFTERS DOUBLE UP AS DECORATION.

left THE LONG, SIMPLE SPACE HAS MERCHANDISE RESTRICTED TO THE SIDE WALLS EXCEPT FOR A METAL SHOE DISPLAY AT THE FAR END.

achieved by careful attention to the actual fabric of the building the shop was moving into. 'The demo process in New York is so interesting that we decided to preserve it,' says Harry Allen. As with the Le Labo shop (see pages 146–149), gutting the space uncovered a series of interesting details, such as different brick and plaster finishes, a door and window that had been covered over and rafters that Allen thought were beautiful.

Allen decided to keep this 'archaeology' and the uncovered details were painted, as part of a very simple concept for the store. The clothes and counter run down the sides of the shop, while the back wall is given over to a black metal display for shoes. This acts as a focal point, and the eye's path to the rear of the store is also guided by large metal ventilation ducting running along the exposed ceiling.

Some bloggers have been critical about the 'tiny' size of the store, while others are scandalized by the fact that the pricey T-shirts aren't available to try on, despite the presence of a changing room. Another element singled out was an über-cool sales assistant too busy acting as a DJ to select friends to do anything other than bark at shoppers touching merchandise they weren't going to buy. Somehow you suspect that this is all intentional theatre, simply reinforcing a sense of aspiration and exclusivity in a sector of the market where these are qualities that many strive after but few attain. Meanwhile, Harry Allen's subtle design ably sets the scene.

HOLTS LAPIDARY

London, UK
Blauel Architects
92m²/990ft²

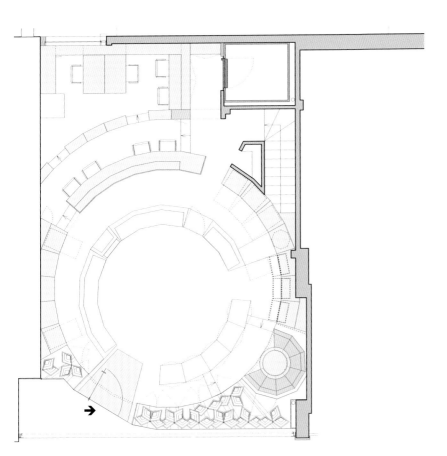

opposite THE FRONT OF THE SHOP PRESENTS JEWELS IN WHAT SEEMS TO BE A LARGE FISSURE IN THE BRUTAL CONCRETE FAÇADE OF THE BUILDING.

left FLOOR PLAN SHOWING THE ARENA-LIKE SPACE ON WHICH THE DESIGN OF THE SHOP IS BASED.

Holts, a family-run jewellers in London that specializes in the cutting, refining and selling of precious stones, while also selling finished jewellery, decided it was time for its business to make a bolder statement to the world.

Brand consultants Walford Wilkie Ltd (then Large Smith Walford) developed a new iridescent logo, suggestive of the gems sold by Holts. They also developed a new retail strategy whereby the general public would be enticed into the store, so that private buyers would supplement Holts' core business, which had been primarily trade customers.

Blauel Architects were then appointed, who developed a design that put the public quite literally at the centre of the shop. Expansion into what had previously been side alleys meant Blauel had the space to come up with a design suggestive of an arena. The main area, likened to an old-fashioned 'trading floor', is surrounded by completely glazed counters full of jewels. It's a space that allows the product to speak while not intimidating the visitor and offering easy browsing.

Customers are surrounded on all sides by the stones, jewellery and staff, in a way that maintains the high level of security required by the value of the merchandise. The arena shape allows for a welcoming and secure space, but also creates an area behind the counters for craftspeople to work on individual pieces while the shop is empty. 'The height means you can't see what is on their desks; this was important for security reasons,' explains Bernhard Blauel. A smaller circular meeting area leads off to provide somewhere for customers to be seated and shown stones or jewellery at leisure.

However, the design's principal gesture is a very public one: a dramatic shopfront suggestive of a large geological fissure. Customers are made to feel as though they are actively discovering the jewels – suspended on trays and intensely lit – inside a crack in a huge piece of rock. Blauel says the inspiration for this gesture was geological rather than architectural, yet the fact that the shop is housed in a heavy, craggy Brutalist concrete building 'meant it had the weight to carry the façade'.

MATERIALS
- Bespoke MDF fittings
- Leather bench
- Iridescent foil

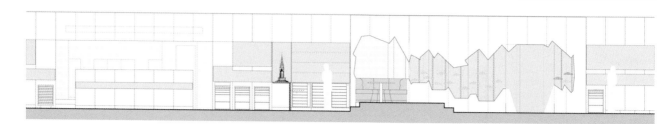

'THE JEWELS ARE SUSPENDED ON TRAYS AND INTENSELY LIT, AS IF INSIDE A CRACK IN A HUGE PIECE OF ROCK.'

Blauel originally intended to build the shopfront in masonry, but planning constraints got in the way. As floor to ceiling glass frontage was required for planning reasons, the feature fissure was instead constructed from MDF and positioned flush to the glass façade. Its fabrication required reliance on a complex concentric geometry. The new foil-based iridescent logo projected well from behind the glass and didn't require the additional glasswork included in early designs. The blue, craggy design of the shopfront was then also adopted as the main visual theme for Holts' website.

Holts is located in Hatton Garden, an area in the City of London that has been associated with jewellers and diamond merchants since the Middle Ages. Past and future come together here in the form of Holts Academy, which trains jewellers-to-be and is located – along with other aspects of the business – on the two floors beneath the main sales floor.

opposite top INTERNAL ELEVATION OF THE STORE.

opposite bottom A CIRCULAR SEATING AREA FOR MORE INTIMATE VIEWINGS AND MEETINGS LEADS OFF THE CENTRAL ARENA.

left THE GEMS AND STONES ARE PRESENTED ON DIFFERENT LEVELS IN THE CRAGGY WINDOW AS IF DISCOVERED IN A GEOLOGICAL FISSURE.

OVERVIEW OF THE CENTRAL ARENA THAT FORMS THE HEART OF THE STORE, WELCOMING THE PUBLIC IN WHILE MAINTAINING SECURE AREAS FOR HOLTS' VALUABLE MERCHANDISE AND ACTIVITIES.

opposite top THE FLAMBOYANT
WINDOW OF EMPEROR MOTH'S MAYFAIR
STORE, REPLETE WITH MOTORIZED AND
CHOREOGRAPHED MANNEQUINS.

opposite bottom FLOOR PLAN OF THE
STORE.

left TWO CONCEPT SKETCHES FOR THE
STORE BY AB ROGERS.

88-93

SMALLER

EMPEROR MOTH

London, UK
Ab Rogers Design
90m²/969ft²

It is difficult to imagine a shop more outrageously flamboyant than Emperor Moth's London store – a hallucinogenic assemblage of mirrors conspire to create an effect that is truly kaleidoscopic. The design was received enthusiastically and reproduced in glossy magazines around the world. 'A crystal palace,' one commentator wittily named it, while another was inspired to emulate the queen in *Snow White* and recite 'mirror, mirror on the wall'.

While a projected store in Moscow didn't happen for planning reasons, Russian fashion designer Katia Gomiashvili turned to Rogers to create a London showcase. She gave him free rein to come up with an energetic, dynamic design to house her collection of clothing – essentially upmarket embroidered tracksuits. The outcome is what Rogers calls a 'mirrored tent'.

'The clothing is very vibrant, so we didn't want to bring in any colour to compete with it,' says Rogers. But this didn't prevent him from choosing a blue floor or deciding that the gaps between the mirrored panels shouldn't

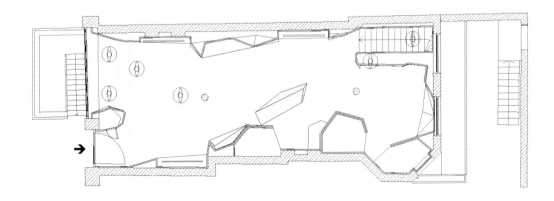

'IT ALL LOOKS BARMY AND IRRATIONAL, BUT IT WAS ACTUALLY ALL COMPUTER-MODELLED.'

be painted in fluorescent pink. Nevertheless, it is the reflections of the clothes, reflecting from one mirror to the next, that provide the store's primary decoration. According to Rogers, they become, in effect, 'the graphics, the wallpaper, the skin that surrounds the space'. Of course, the visitor too becomes part of the decoration as he or she tours the space.

The mirrors are mounted on an MDF backing, and each mirror panel is removable. 'It all looks barmy and irrational, but it was actually all computer-modelled,' says Rogers, adding that the result is largely down to the skills of Dutch shopfitter Harry Van Rooij. One source of inspiration for the mirrors was the work of the artist Robert Smithson. The store's other aspect – its population of absurd, colourful, fantastical creatures – was inspired by the esoteric mosaic sculptures made by French artist Niki de Saint Phalle for her famous Tarot Garden in Tuscany.

In the store, humanized hangers seem to be biting the clothes rail on which they hang, while animated mannequin puppets jump up and down in the window, choreographed by Dominic Robson. 'There was a fear that it would be cold and hard with all those mirrors,' says Rogers. He needn't have worried, although it's a space more introverted individuals may want to give a wide berth.

MATERIALS
- Glass and poly-
  carbonate mirrors
  on MDF
- Motorized,
  choreographed
  mannequins
- Blue resin floor

PHILIPPE DUBUC

Montreal, Canada
Saucier + Perrotte Architectes
90m²/969ft²

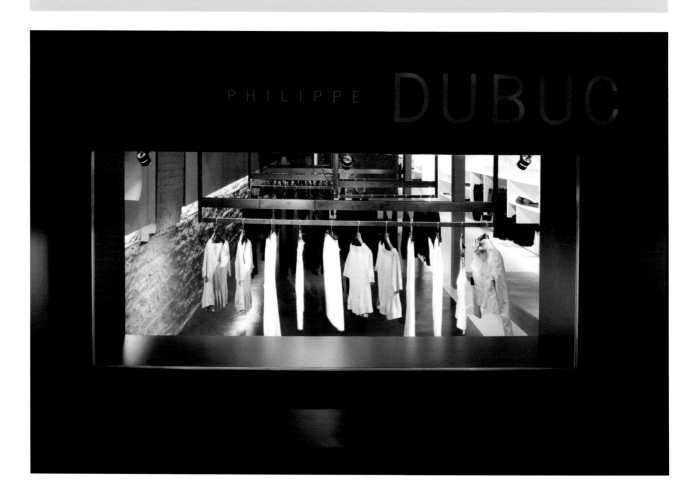

opposite top LOOKING DOWN INTO THE STORE FROM THE STREET THROUGH A HEAVY METAL WINDOW, THE VIEWER SEES THE CLOTHING HANGING FROM AUSTERE RAILS.

opposite bottom CONCEPT SKETCH OF THE FLOOR PLAN, SHOWING THE SUBDIVISION OF THE SPACE INTO BLACK-AND-WHITE HALVES.

below FLOOR PLAN. 1/ENTRANCE, 2/RAMP, 3/WHITE LACQUERED SHELVING, 4/SLIDING CLOTHES HANGING SYSTEMS, 5/FITTING ROOMS.

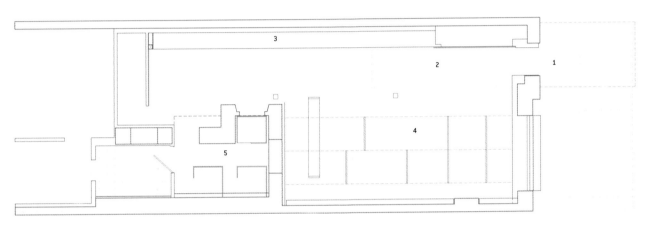

MATERIALS
- Black steel window frame
- Raw concrete
- Painted stone
- Tinted glass
- White lacquered shelves
- Yellow-painted wood panelling

As you walk past this shopfront, its black steel surround – substantial and stern in appearance – frames your view down into the store. There you see clothes arranged on austere, ceiling-mounted steel rails, as if on a production line of ghosts.

The boutique, created for Philippe Dubuc (one of Canada's leading fashion designers) by Montreal-based practice Saucier + Perrotte, is a store of two halves. You enter the first, right-hand, half by proceeding down a long entrance ramp. The ramp takes up nearly half the length of the boutique, but a mirror at the end of the store makes the space seem to extend, preventing any suggestion of claustrophobia.

Apart from the raw concrete ramp, this first half is entirely white, from the floor right up to the irregular, white-lacquered shelving. In contrast, the left-hand side, where the clothes rails that you can see from the outside hang, is largely black. A rough, exposed stone wall provides a textural contrast with the glossy shelving of the other half.

The architects refer to their approach as an 'invented archaeology' in which found elements, such as the exposed stone wall that was already there, are supplemented by other features, some obviously new and others seemingly unearthed. 'The assemblage of historic and new elements, seemingly unearthed along with the built form, results in a superimposition of many eras of the building's life,' according to the architects.

The single yellow highlight provided by the painted wood of the fitting rooms breaks the rigid, chessboard-like black and white of the store. The overall effect is austere modernism with an intriguing twist. Despite suffering financial troubles and eventual bankruptcy, Dubuc managed to keep hold of this, his flagship store.

left A REFLECTION OF YELLOW-PAINTED WOOD FROM THE FITTING ROOMS, WHICH PROVIDE THE ONLY ACCENT OF COLOUR IN THE OTHERWISE CHEQUERBOARD BLACK-AND-WHITE STORE.

below FLOOR-LEVEL VIEW OF THE STORE FROM UNDER THE CLOTHES RAILS, SHOWING THE ENTRANCE RAMP.

opposite THE DESIGN RESTS HEAVILY ON THE DISTINCTION BETWEEN THE WHITE AND BLACK HALVES OF THE STORE.

'THE ASSEMBLAGE OF HISTORIC AND NEW ELEMENTS, SEEMINGLY UNEARTHED ALONG WITH THE BUILT FORM, RESULTS IN A SUPERIMPOSITION OF MANY ERAS OF THE BUILDING'S LIFE.'

left A MANNEQUIN STANDS BETWEEN
CONTRASTING LACQUERED SHELVES AND
THE HEAVILY TEXTURED ROUGH WALLS.

below and bottom ELEVATION AND
PHOTOGRAPHIC DETAIL OF THE WHITE
LACQUERED SHELVES THAT DOMINATE
THE RIGHT-HAND WALL OF THE STORE.

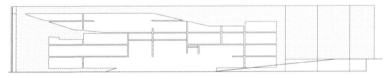

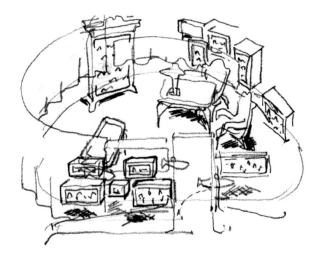

'A cabinet of curiosities, imbued with a magical domestic touch.' That's how Nigel Coates describes his design for Charles Fish, a long-established jeweller in the East End of London. Fish was looking for a new kind of jewellery store, and a design that would be strong enough to form the basis of a future roll-out.

For this first store, located in Canary Wharf, the client and its brand consultants decided they wanted something that would combine innovation and tradition. They also settled on two particular aspects that they felt should be part of the mix: there had to be 'something watery' to marry up with the company name, and they wanted the design to be eclectic. 'I'm never quite sure how to interpret eclectic,' says Coates. 'So I thought of it as diverse cultural influences brought together to create a harmonious whole.' And the result here was the unlikely combination of rococo style and underwater landscape.

Central to the concept is a play between big and small and between new and old. 'Some of the furniture was old, some we had made, so you are never quite sure,'

100-105
SMALLER

CHARLES FISH
London, UK
Branson Coates
80m²/861ft²

says Coates. The shop window has been conceived as a kind of fish tank, allowing tantalizing glimpses into the store, which opens up when the customer enters. Inside, jewellery is presented on sinewy, seaweed-like shapes, contrasting with strong, rectilinear boxes for the watches.

Hanging from the ceiling are giant, shell-like shapes, made from foam and fibreglass using boat-building techniques. 'You might argue that they make a small space seem smaller but I think that by making the edges shadowy they actually make it seem bigger,' says Coates. A black chair by Dutch designer Maarten Baas sits in one corner, clearly chosen for its ambiguous status between new and old. Budget restraints meant that a melamine counter was what Coates terms an 'hommage à Fornasetti' rather than the real thing.

The Medusa chandelier, with its jellyfish-like shape, was designed by Coates specifically for this store, but has since been put into production by Italian company Slamp. It hangs over a bespoke table that somehow combines rococo and glass-bottomed boat.

opposite TWO CONCEPT SKETCHES OF THE STORE BY NIGEL COATES.

left THE STORE IS FURNISHED WITH AN ECLECTIC RANGE OF PIECES, INCLUDING THIS DISTRESSED GLASS-TOPPED DISPLAY TABLE.

left THE MEDUSA CHANDELIER WAS DESIGNED FOR THIS STORE BUT HAS SINCE BEEN PUT INTO PRODUCTION.

opposite top DETAIL OF SOME OF THE BOUDOIR-LIKE DECORATION OF THE STORE.

opposite bottom THE GEOMETRIC DISPLAY CASES FOR THE WATCHES CONTRASTS WITH THE SINEWY SHAPES AND FURNISHINGS OF THE STORE.

'SOME OF THE FURNITURE WAS OLD, SOME WE HAD MADE, SO YOU ARE NEVER QUITE SURE.'

left A FORNASETTI-ESQUE COUNTER, CEILING-MOUNTED GIANT CLAM SHELLS (MADE FROM FIBREGLASS) AND FISH-TANK DISPLAYS MAKE FOR AN UNUSUAL RETAIL ENVIRONMENT.

below THE BRANDING FOR THE STORE, CREATED BY WALFORD WILKIE, WAS A STARTING POINT FOR THE SURREAL AND PLAYFUL INTERIOR DESIGN BY NIGEL COATES.

charles fish

MATERIALS
- 'Smoke' armchair by Maarten Baas
- 'Medusa' chandelier by Nigel Coates
- Fibreglass shells made using boat-building techniques

EKO

Toronto, Canada
Bennett C. Lo, dialogue 38
80m²/861ft²

eko

From the outside, what you see of EKO's interior is a white, shimmering cube, whose ribs concertina backwards around a spine of marble. It's an approach that the project's designers, Dialogue 38, admit is designed to pique curiosity and play a game of hide-and-seek with shoppers and passers-by. It is also an approach that merges genres – if a white cube suggests a gallery space rather than a shop, then that fits well with the limited edition, hand-crafted jewellery from around the world that EKO sells.

But to see the merchandise, other than that draped around a solitary window mannequin, you need to go inside the store and investigate the spaces between the white ribs, to discover the 'hidden treasures'. There, behind glass rather than the usual apparatus of shelves, you find the jewellery ingeniously displayed on white magnetic aluminium blocks. It's a flexible system that allows the display to be easily rearranged.

Looking in from outside, the cantilevered marble table at the centre of the space seems to float. Leading the

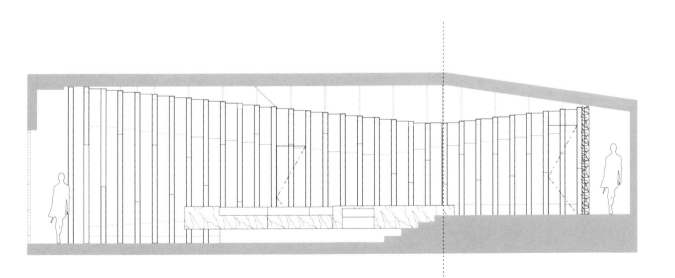

eye to the back of the interior, it also conceals the cash counter. The rear wall is given over to displays by local artists, and as their work rotates, it is allowed to impart a different visual flavour to the space. And, of course, it further endorses the store's aspiration to become a gallery space. For the shop's opening, the rear wall was given over to an installation by Dialogue 38's principal, Bennett C. Lo, and his client, Mina Yoon, an old friend.

The highly controlled design of the store manages to pull off a very difficult act. Once it has done its work in being eye-catching enough to draw passers-by in, it then performs just as well as an effective and neutral display vehicle for the jewellery on sale.

Located in Toronto's Queen West district, EKO had been in existence since 2000 but needed a revamp in the face of fresh competition. For the renovation, completed at the end of 2006, the store's small footprint of 54 square metres (580 square feet) was enlarged to 80 square metres (861 square feet) by extending into what had previously been a storeroom at the back. The receding

white ribs, made of MDF and bunching two thirds of the way into the interior, create a perspective effect that makes the store seem bigger than it really is.

right THE CANTILEVERED MARBLE TABLE ACTS AS THE SPINE OF THE STORE AND CONCEALS ITS MAIN DESK.

opposite VIEW FROM INSIDE THE STORE THROUGH ITS MINIMAL GLASS FRONT TO THE STREET OUTSIDE.

'YOU NEED TO GO INSIDE THE STORE AND INVESTIGATE THE SPACES BETWEEN THE WHITE RIBS TO DISCOVER THE "HIDDEN TREASURES".'

When the cultural and design history of the early twenty-first century is written, a certain style, be it for shop, club or bar, will loom large. This is a confident, slick and glamorous look where soft edges and shiny surfaces abound. It is a style that references, and seeks to partake of the glamour of, Italian design of the 1960s. At the very beginning of the twenty-first century this seemed part of a ubiquitous retro obsession in design. However, with the passing of years, it seems very rooted in – and expressive of – its own historical moment.

In retail, one could point to the environments that William Russell, now at Pentagram, developed for Alexander McQueen's boutiques around the world. Or the Marni stores, designed first by Future Systems, and then by breakaway design group Sybarite. Both typify the nightclub-like retro glamour of the genre. But perhaps it is a style that had its quintessential expression in the Korean boutique of Parisian fashion designer Martine Sitbon.

MARTINE SITBON

Seoul, Korea
Moongyu Choi, Ga.a Architects; Mass Studies; Slade Architecture
69m²/743ft²

'TWO-WAY MIRROR GLASS MEANT THE
UPPER PART WOULD DRAMATICALLY
REFLECT THE SKY.'

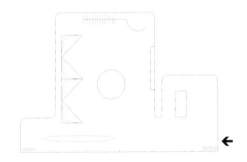

Designed by Cho Slade, made up of a group of designers who have all since gone their separate ways, the store selling women's fashion was basically a makeover of a former bar. Its unusual location is inside a residential villa in what had only recently become a prime commercial part of town. The store is dominated by an enormous glass wall, 7.2 metres (23$\frac{1}{2}$ feet) high. Two-way mirror glass for the top half of the wall meant that during the day this upper part would dramatically reflect the sky, while the bottom half allows you to see inside. At night, the glass at the top would stop reflecting and glow instead, an effect facilitated by roughly back-painting the glass with polyester.

This glass wall defined the shop, which the designers likened to a giant aquarium. The entire shop was rendered a window display; everything inside seemed to float in an interior 'reskinned' in such a way, say the designers, that there were only smoothed, rounded surfaces 'as if they were cast in plastic from a single mould' or 'injected with botox'. It is a look that received its tactile equivalent with a 'squishy' shop counter made of silicon.

While the floor area may be small, in its ambitions the store was as huge as its glass frontage. However, Sitbon and her Korean backers suffered various financial problems after the opening, which sealed the fate of the store which was then closed. Sitbon returned to the world of fashion some years later, setting up in business again – this time as creative director of her company Rue du Mail, as she no longer owned her own name.

SOFT, MOULDED, SEAMLESS SHAPES
DOMINATE THE STORE, AS IF INJECTED
WITH BOTOX.

HUNT & GATHER

Vancouver, Canada
Natalie Purschwitz
*c.*65m²/700ft² including workshop

right VIEW THROUGH THE WINDOW, SHOWING THE CHROME-PAINTED TREE BRANCHES ON WHICH THE CLOTHES ARE HUNG.

Like many fashion designers, Natalie Purschwitz had very clear ideas about what she wanted from her store. She also had the confidence to design it herself. As well as an enticing space for potential customers, it would have to accommodate her workshop. So sewing machines and a cutting table are there without, Purschwitz hopes, intruding on the controlled aesthetic of the store.

The shop is a work in progress, morphing with the different collections of clothing she designs, as well as functioning as an occasional, ad hoc exhibition space. And rather than the usual fashion references, Purschwitz chose readily identifiable Canadian elements to give a distinct flavour to her store.

As a result, very traditional and rustic, even primeval, elements are given a surprising but highly controlled makeover — always, however, in a way that would complement her clothing designs. 'I started juxtaposing natural materials with man-made, taking the best attributes of both and combining them,' says Purschwitz.

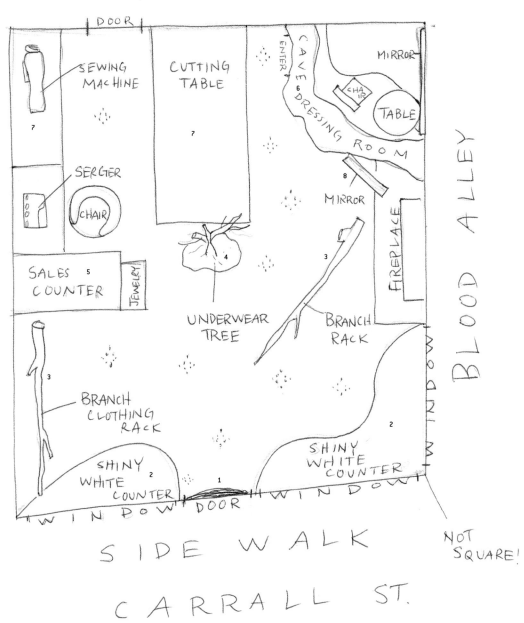

HUNT + GATHER
FLOOR PLAN   * NOT TO SCALE!

DOOR

SEWING MACHINE

CUTTING TABLE

CAVE DRESSING ROOM

ENTER

MIRROR

CHAIR

TABLE

7

7

6

8

SERGER

CHAIR

MIRROR

3

BLOOD ALLEY

SALES COUNTER

JEWELRY

5

UNDERWEAR TREE

4

BRANCH RACK

FIREPLACE

3

BRANCH CLOTHING RACK

3

2

WINDOW

SHINY WHITE COUNTER

2

SHINY WHITE COUNTER

2

1

WINDOW   DOOR   WINDOW

NOT SQUARE!

S I D E   W A L K

C A R R A L L   S T.

opposite FLOOR PLAN. 1/ENTRANCE, 2/SHINY WHITE COUNTERS, 3/BRANCH CLOTHING RACKS, 4/'UNDERWEAR TREE', 5/SALES COUNTER, 6/PAPIER-MÂCHÉ 'CAVE' CHANGING ROOM, 7/CUTTING TABLES AND SEWING AREA, 8/MIRROR.

below THE 'UNDERWEAR TREE' AT THE CENTRE OF THE IMAGE IS USED TO DISPLAY LINGERIE.

below left AN EERIE TAXIDERMIST'S MODEL OF A COUGAR SITS ON A TABLE IN FRONT OF THE BESPOKE WALLPAPER DERIVED FROM TRADITIONAL COLUMBIAN POSTERS.

'For example, a branch is chrome-painted and used as a rack for hanging clothes because the form is already beautiful but then the man-made element takes it out of context enough to see the shape in a new way.'

It's a quirky combination that runs throughout the store, from the typography of the Hunt & Gather logotype (designed by local outfit Max & Hadley) to the igloo in the corner, which is actually a papier-mâché 'cave' in which customers can try on clothes. This is furnished with a mirror and chair and is, unsurprisingly, a popular feature of the store.

A deer's head looms out from a wall and, adding a slightly sinister touch, a cougar (puma) mannequin sits atop a table. 'It's the form that a taxidermist would use under the hide of the animal,' explains Purschwitz. 'That's why it's a little creepy, because it doesn't have any ears or paws or defined features.'

As well as the wilderness aspect, Canadian heritage of a different kind is celebrated in the store. For instance, the back wall is given over to wallpaper designed by

the artist Jenifer Papararo, a member of local collective Instant Coffee. 'She had the wallpaper made in Columbia in the form of posters. These are ubiquitous in Columbia for advertising and making announcements. They are printed using oil-based inks on newsprint with letterpress printing presses but they usually have a limited number of typesetting dies. Jenifer asked the printer to use all of the Os and Os that he had that were over a certain size. To preserve the aesthetic we chose to install the posters in the traditional style,' explains Purschwitz.

Located in the historic Gastown area of Vancouver, Hunt & Gather is in a building that had once been a hotel. 'My space is the only one in the building that still has the original floor,' says Purschwitz. 'I really like to blend old and new, traditional and contemporary.'

above THE ORIGINAL FIN-DE-SIÈCLE
MOSAIC FLOOR WAS RETAINED, STILL
BEARING THE NAME OF THE BODEGA
HOTEL.

opposite LITTLE BIRDS SIT ATOP THE
PAPIER-MÂCHÉ 'CAVE' IN THE CORNER
WHICH FUNCTIONS AS THE CHANGING
ROOM.

'I STARTED JUXTAPOSING NATURAL MATERIALS WITH MAN-MADE, TAKING THE BEST ATTRIBUTES OF BOTH AND COMBINING THEM.'

MATERIALS
- Papier-mâché changing room
- Taxidermist's dolls
- Chrome-painted tree branches
- Wallpaper hand-printed with oil-based dyes

ELS█ CHAPEAUX
ACCESSOIRES S
ACS FOULARDS
CEINTURES BRA
CELETS COLLIE
RS BAGUES ELS

ELSA BIJOUX

Madrid, Spain
Teresa Sapey Estudio de Arquitectura
61 m²/657 ft²

NTURONES SO
BREROS PULSE
AS ANILLOS B
CHES ELSA BI
U ACCESSO

'THE GRAPHICS ARE PRESENTED TWO- AND THREE-DIMENSIONALLY AND IN GENEROUS PROPORTIONS.'

Words, words, words. That's what you get when you get to Elsa Bijoux, a women's fashion accessories store in Madrid. For their French client, Teresa Sapey's architectural practice decided that graphics should be the mainstay of the design, with words in a bold sans serif font (AG Schoolbook, in case you're wondering) listing the wares on sale wherever you look.

Words greet customers straight away: the cast-iron main door is punctured with words, like a giant stencil, creating interesting light effects for the shop's interior. Rather than being cut out, the graphics inside the store are presented two- and three-dimensionally and in generous proportions. The list of accessories can be discerned in faint letters on a wall of shiny, transparent vinyl but on another wall, on the right-hand side of the store, giant lettering juts out in 3-D.

These 3-D letters are attached to what initially seems a wall but is, in fact, an integrated storage system, featuring drawers and cabinets made of lacquered MDF.

The only free-standing unit is a glass-topped table display
in the centre of the store.

Two recessed areas in vivid yellow and orange provide
a contrast to the pristine white of the lettering and the
rest of the store. These shiny, coloured surfaces of the
recessed areas also provide a contrast in texture to the
white of the walls, the three-dimensional lettering and
the cabinets. A hatch made of reinforced coloured glass
conceals a staircase going down to the basement.

The graphics-heavy approach is one that Teresa Sapey
had also used for the car park of Madrid's Hotel Puerta
America, for which many of the world's most famous
architects and designers created different floors or
elements.

left THE RECESSED AREAS OF THE CABINETS ARE FINISHED IN REFLECTIVE RED OR YELLOW.

MATERIALS
- Laquered MDF
- Cast-iron door
- Transparent, shiny
  vinyl wall finish

LIL SHOP
Berlin, Germany
Lil Schlichting-Stegemann
60m²/646ft²

left THE UNASSUMING EXTERIOR OF THE LIL SHOP IN BERLIN'S MITTE AREA.

opposite THE COMIC WALLPAPER DESIGNED BY THOMAS ZEITLBERGER DOMINATES THE VIEW OF THE STORE FROM OUTSIDE.

After establishing the first three, very influential, 'Guerrilla Stores' for Comme des Garçons in Berlin, Lil Schlichting-Stegemann decided it was time for the fourth incarnation to be a little less peripatetic and to have a single, fixed home. As the concept had shifted slightly – no longer were they upping and moving sticks from one existing retail space to another with minimal intervention – the shop needed to have a different name. Given the small dimensions of the new site in Berlin's Mitte district and Schlichting-Stegemann's first name, the store was duly christened Lil Shop.

'The store had previously been a gallery,' she explains. 'It was a bit boring, a bit pure. I wanted a bit of atmosphere.' She discussed her ideas with a Viennese artist friend of hers, Thomas Zeitlberger, whose day job is a designer for Austrian television, and they came up with the concept that she describes as 'a rococo salon, with soft baroque decoration yet with a comic attitude'.

It was Zeitlberger who designed the wallpaper, which plays with baroque motifs such as trompe l'oeil panels

right THE STORE USES FURNITURE SOURCED FROM LOCAL FLEA MARKETS, SUCH AS THIS WARDROBE.

opposite CLOTHING IS HUNG ON A FOLDING SCREEN THAT ALLOWS THE SPACE TO BE CONTINUALLY RECONFIGURED.

MATERIALS
- Antique and vintage flea market furniture
- Bespoke wallpaper by Thomas Zeitlberger
- Fluorescent strip lighting

'IF WE DON'T LIKE SOMETHING WE CAN JUST CHUCK IT OUT AND FIND SOMETHING ELSE IN THE FLEA MARKET.'

depicting birds and foliage, and disrupts the experience by interspersing unexpected items such as a vacuum cleaner. Schlichting-Stegemann says the wallpaper has the unexpected consequence of making the space feel bigger than it did when painted white.

As with the previous Comme des Garçons Guerrilla Stores, Schlichting-Stegemann sourced furniture herself from flea markets. So a rococo chair with busily embroidered upholstery sits next to baroque furniture that has been painted white, along with perfunctory items such as reclaimed clothes rails. A 1950s entertainment centre was gutted of its TV and stereo to make way for the store's computer.

'The idea is to keep it changing and keep it flexible. If we couldn't change the location as with the Guerrilla Stores, at least we could keep on changing the interior. It isn't so much a design as creating a space that wasn't stiff and boring,' she says. 'If we don't like something we can just chuck it out and find something else in the flea market. This makes it interesting for the customer and also for

left MERCHANDISE IS SIMPLY DISPLAYED
ON A VARIETY OF SECOND-HAND TABLES,
CABINETS AND RAILS, AND IS LIT BY
PERFUNCTORY FLUORESCENT STRIPS.

me. Remember, unlike most fashion shops, we don't just
get big deliveries four times a year.'

A movable wall helps the store to adopt different
characters at different times, as well as providing a
space for a changing room. The floor was left as it was
and simple fluorescent lighting was used. The approach
allows the clothing to remain centre stage at all times,
and in any case the continually changing product
— Comme des Garçons supplies a mixture of vintage,
current and special-edition clothing on a monthly basis
— ensures that the store is never static.

CAMPER MILAN

Milan, Italy
Jaime Hayón with Studio Camper
54m²/581ft²

opposite THE VIEW FROM THE BACK OF THE STORE OUT TO THE STREET IS DOMINATED BY A SURREALLY OVERSIZED RED LAMPSHADE.

below left and right THE SHOP WINDOWS ARE FRAMED WITH PLAYFUL SILHOUETTED ILLUSTRATIONS.

If there is any brand that can be described as a specialist in small-store design, it is Mallorcan shoe brand Camper. Eschewing the cookie-cutter school of global branding, where the first commandment is that everything should look the same, all Camper's stores are different. A raft of distinguished designers have been given free reign to reconsider what a small shoe shop could look like, and the quirky, individualistic design of the shops has managed to be a much more subtle enforcer of a sense of brand than any bland standardization.

At their best, Camper's shoe shops sometimes appear to be test beds for innovative design as much as spaces for selling shoes. It is a strategy that started out with the input of Spanish designers such as Javier Mariscal and Martí Guixé. But Camper has added to its portfolio with work by current stars of the design scene. Brazilian brothers Humberto and Fernando Campana designed a shop for Camper in Berlin, Swiss designer Alfredo Häberli one in Paris, and Jaime Hayón is responsible for

a series of five shops in Palma de Mallorca, Paris, London, Barcelona and Milan.

The Camper stores were the first foray of Hayón's digital baroque style into the field of interior design. All five are united by a common concept and the strong individuality of Hayón's style, the impact of which is perhaps clearest in the Milan store. Oversize red and gold lights suspended from the ceiling create a fairy-tale environment that manages to feel intriguing and inviting rather than make the small space seem crowded. The presentation of the shoes on tables is simultaneously simple and practical, with a slightly surreal flavour. The shop furniture is just that, with an unpredictable and luscious twist.

As a Spaniard, Hayón grew up with the brand and therefore didn't need to have too tight a brief, says Dalia Saliamonas, Camper's creative director. 'Instantly there was a good vibe and Hayón was given free rein,' she adds.

Saliamonas wanted a concept that would adapt to fit the different sizes of the shops (none was more than 100

square metres/1,076 square feet) and that would 'create a warm and creative image in the limited space, as well as adhere to the retail needs in terms of display, cash register, lighting'.

Saliamonas describes the result as a shop that is also 'a gallery with exclusive pieces designed just for the project'. For example, the tables are Hayón creations with mismatched legs that, while exclusive to the shop, are part of a series. 'Each piece of furniture was studied, adapted and individualized for each shop,' explains Saliamonas.

The lamps are made from clay and porcelain, which she sees as 'creating an updated Mediterranean feel'. Likewise, the theatrical red-and-white chequered floor references baroque style in a contemporary way while also unambiguously alluding to Camper's brand identity.

While Hayón was responsible for the concept of the store, the final drawings and execution, including technical aspects such as lighting, were overseen by the in-house design team, Studio Camper.

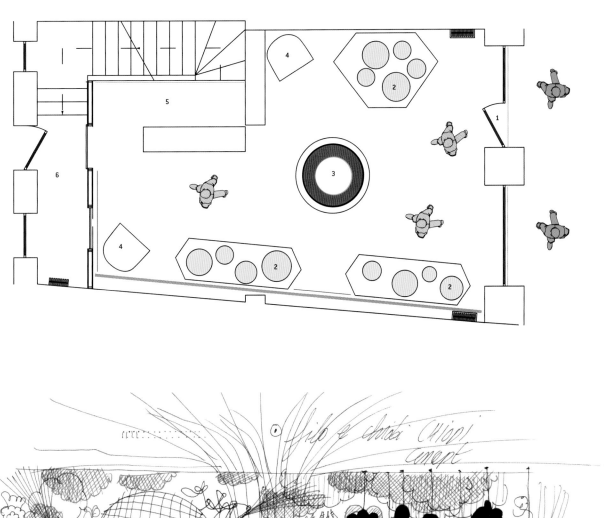

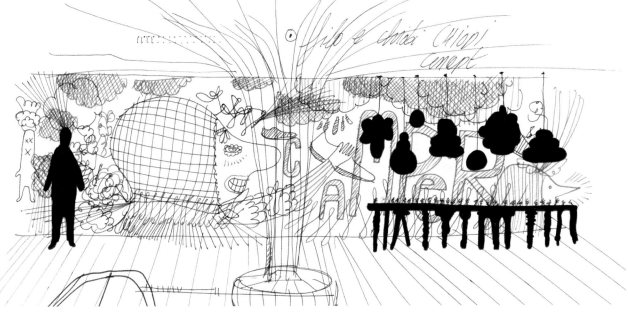

this page GOLD, CERAMIC AND RED-CLOTH LAMP SHADES DOMINATE THE SPACE, WHILE THE DISTINCTIVE FURNITURE IS ENTIRELY WHITE.

opposite CAMPER'S BRANDING LENT THE INTERIOR DESIGN ITS OVERALL COLOUR SCHEME.

MATERIALS
- Bespoke furniture created to Hayón's designs by project architect Belloni and other suppliers
- Porcelain and clay suspension lighting

'THERE WAS A GOOD VIBE AND HAYÓN WAS GIVEN FREE REIN.'

When Aranaz, a Philippine handbag brand, asked young designer Juan Carlo Calma, fresh from studying architecture in the UK, to design a store that mimicked the reflective surface of their products, they surely must have got a little bit more than they bargained for. Not only does the small store reproduce some of the elements of a crocodile-skin evening bag, but it also gives you the unusual feeling of having walked right inside one.

Calma says his design took as its departure the skins of exotic animals such as crocodiles and their 'tessellated geometry'. 'The overall concept was to create a skin assemblage that wraps around the store and provides integrated shelving, lighting and product display,' explains Calma. 'The crocodile-skin-inspired wall is made of recycled timber faces and then scored laminates were put on top. It was prefabricated off site, and is composed of 220 pieces – it's easy-assembly, flat-packed and has a low carbon footprint.'

Calma claims that the intricate ceiling, with its many

'IT GIVES YOU THE UNUSUAL FEELING OF HAVING WALKED RIGHT INSIDE A CROCODILE HANDBAG.'

142-145
SMALLER

ARANAZ BOUTIQUE
Makati City, Philippines
Juan Carlo Calma
52m²/560ft²

slits, creates graduated microclimates and works as an acoustic element. 'The configuration of ceiling acoustic panels produces multi-directional sound reflections from the variably sized and angled surfaces, creating a diffuse sound-landscape within the retail space,' he says.

Executed on a shoestring budget of £14,000 ($28,000), the store is in a shopping centre in Makati City, one of the metropolitan districts of Manila, capital of the Philippines. The store continually changes, via new installations and different featured bags, and it has a special room at the back of the boutique for clients who wish to have bespoke designs created for them, including bags from their own designs.

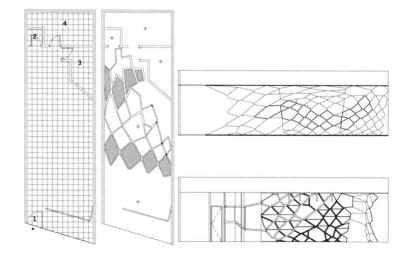

left THE 'TESSELLATED GEOMETRY' OF EXOTIC ANIMAL SKINS WAS THE INSPIRATION FOR THE STORE'S INTRICATE DESIGN.

above SIMPLE AND CHEAP MATERIALS SUCH AS RECYCLED TIMBER AND VINYL FLOOR TILES ARE USED FOR THE STORE.

MATERIALS
- Recycled timber
- Scored formica laminates in metallic rosewood for crocodile effect on walls and ceiling
- Vinyl reflective floor tiles

LE LABO

New York, New York, USA
Eddie Roschi and Fabrice Penot with Auric Consultancy + Design
50m²/538ft²

MATERIALS
- Restored tin wall finished in silver
- Vintage cast-iron tables
- White brick tiles
- Furniture from local antique shops
- Distressed wood floors

opposite THE ENTRANCE TO LE LABO'S NEW YORK STORE, SHOWING THE DELIBERATELY ROUGH AND READY STENCILLED GRAPHICS.

below A BAR OFFERING PERFUME RATHER THAN DRINK FORMS THE STORE'S CENTREPIECE. ITS AMBIENCE COMES FROM A MIXTURE OF RESTORED FEATURES AND LOCALLY SOURCED SECOND-HAND FURNITURE.

Walk up to the bar in Le Labo and, rather than a Martini, you ask for perfume – handmade to order. Located in Manhattan's NoLita district, Le Labo is the brainchild of founders Eddie Roschi and Fabrice Penot, who professed themselves fed up with the mass-produced global perfume business and its ubiquitous brands. Their idea was to offer a bespoke service where customers could order fragrances blended freshly on the spot to preselected recipes.

When demolition work started on this, their first shop, the pair started off by seeing what was really there, and discovered a tin wall under layers of redecoration on the left wall. 'This is something typical for New York and we decided to keep it and make it a feature,' says Roschi. As it was in a poor state, the tin was gently renovated so that it wouldn't seem overrestored, and then finished in silver. They were so happy with this feature that it has been replicated for the other stores that followed in its footsteps (in Los Angeles and Tokyo), to confer both a sense of brand continuity and also a New York vibe.

above THE EXISTING TIN WALL WAS
RESTORED AND FINISHED IN SILVER.

The use of white brick tiles was a feature similarly evocative of New York's visual heritage and furniture was sourced from local antique shops. Distressed wood was used for the flooring, and the perfume sampling area is furnished with vintage cast-iron tables.

Right from the beginning, the founders were determined that the store should look 'lived in and old'. They developed the design by themselves 'on the hoof' but enlisted the help of local consultancy Auric Consultancy + Design for its implementation.

The last thing Le Labo's founders wanted was a conspicuously 'designed' store. Instead they arrived at something Roschi hopes 'feels old and genuine', where nothing is superfluous. As Le Labo is all about having your perfume made up to order ('unlike wine, perfume ages poorly,' says Roschi), too slick a store would have been inappropriate and also too close to the globalized, standardized perfume business to which Le Labo offers an alternative. To this end, the branding and packaging has a similarly provisional quality.

below VINTAGE CAST-IRON TABLES WERE
SOURCED FOR THE PERFUME SAMPLING
AREA.

bottom LE LABO'S OTHER STORES, SUCH
AS THIS ONE IN TOKYO, RETAIN CERTAIN
FEATURES FROM THE INAUGURAL NEW
YORK STORE.

'TOO SLICK A STORE WOULD HAVE BEEN INAPPROPRIATE.'

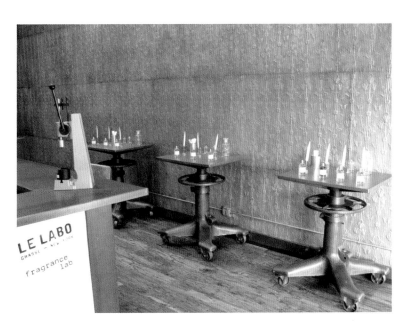

M.Y. LABEL

Tokyo, Japan
Masamichi Katayama, Wonderwall
50m²/538ft²

opposite THE VIEW FROM OUTSIDE IS SO INSCRUTABLE THAT PASSERS-BY WOULD BE HARD PUSHED TO GUESS THIS IS A JEWELLERY STORE.

left INTERIOR MATERIALS, SUCH AS EXPOSED CONCRETE, ARE LEFT TO SPEAK FOR THEMSELVES.

Despite appearances, M.Y. Label is a jewellery store that only sells items that have been designed in-house. It takes its name from the initials of the store's creative director, Maki Yoshida, who happens to be a personal friend of Masamichi Katayama, founder of acclaimed Japanese interior design firm Wonderwall. And it was to Wonderwall that Yoshida turned for M.Y. Label's first, and exceptionally discreet, flagship store.

If Toronto jewellery store EKO (see pages 106–111) plays games of 'hide and seek' to entice customers in, Katayama's design for M.Y. Label takes the concept to a greater extreme. From the outside, the storefront signage is self-effacing to the point of being unnoticeable and does little to tell you what you are looking at.

The design of the interior, an inscrutable assemblage of highly controlled surfaces, supplies no further clues, and certainly none of the standard retail cues. Materials used here, including unpainted concrete walls, speak for themselves alone. Is it an office? A meeting room of an advertising agency? A private home?

above and opposite A CENTRAL MEETING TABLE DOMINATES IN THE EXCEPTIONALLY DISCREET STORE DESIGN, WHICH IS GIVEN A SUBTLE TWIST BY THE REFLECTIONS IN THE LARGE MIRROR AND GLASS CABINETS.

'IT WAS IMPORTANT TO CREATE A SENSE OF DISCOVERY.'

A round table takes up the centre of the internal space, surrounded by four of Charles and Ray Eames' classic and ubiquitous Aluminium Group office chairs, here upholstered in a muted grey. Behind it, resting at an angle against the wall, is a large mirror. To the side is a curious glass object that turns out to be a display counter and chest of drawers. Apart from a narrow, glass-covered display at the top, it is really only when these drawers are opened that M.Y. Label's merchandise, the jewellery, is seen.

Despite a sober general impression, this store's design is actually one of maximum theatre. The elegant sobriety only accentuates the drama of the drawers finally being opened to reveal the merchandise, or of the jewellery being brought to the central 'meeting table'.

Katayama explains the project as follows: 'M.Y. Label creates simple and elegant jewellery with a very high level of craftsmanship. It was important to design a store that would not only complement the jewellery but also create a sense of discovery. I imagined an atelier-like space void of decorativeness with the emphasis on solid materials. I also wanted to create an atmosphere devised specially to work with the customers and to provide a sense of exploration by not having all the merchandise readily visible; only giving a glimpse of the pieces as the drawers under the glass counter tops are being pulled open.'

MATERIALS
• Charles and Ray Eames 'Aluminium Group' office chairs by Vitra
• Unpainted concrete

TINY

INTERVIEW
STEVE LIDBURY

Steve Lidbury is a British designer who now has his base in Japan after cutting his teeth at Fabrica, the design centre established by Benetton in Italy. His studio is multidisciplinary but is recognized for its retail designs. Wide-ranging projects include boutiques such as the flagship store for fashion designer Sunao Kawahara and shops like the Smacky Glam chain, which targets young office women.

What is it about small shops that appeals to you as a designer? I think the principal factor is that a small shop has a more bespoke quality to it. I do a variety of different projects – some are very small while others are 20-shop roll-outs. If you have a smaller space you can customize everything in there, from the whole internal structure down to very bespoke furniture details. It allows you to get your teeth into every aspect of the design: lighting, materials, furniture and so on. Of course you do all those things anyway, but in a small shop you are just able to give more attention to them.

Would doing a large store like Uniqlo appeal as much as designing a boutique? There are a lot of restrictions with these kinds of projects. But Masamichi Katayama of Wonderwall has shown what you can do. The vending machine idea that he uses for Uniqlo is very interesting and shows you can create interesting concepts with bigger shops and with a plain brand. So it is not so much the size of the project, but more about the client and how much risk they are willing to take with the design.

You use a lot of oblique angles in your shops – is that a response to some of the formal problems when designing small shops? Well, it is about breaking the existing geometry. What I try to achieve is to create a different world within a small space. The shops are often in a complex that houses lots of other brands and where there are a lot of other things going on. By breaking the existing geometry the consumer is then almost exploring another world. But this does pose a challenge with a small space, as it isn't easy to break it up into a series of even smaller spaces.

So do you try and make small shops seem bigger than they really are? Yes, I think the key with a small space is to try and make it feel bigger than it is. Something you will notice in my shops is the use of mirrors. It sounds banal to say that the use of mirrors can make the shop seem twice as big as it really is, but with mirrors, glass and reflections you can create wonders. You really can make the space feel a lot bigger, and in a restrained way so that you don't produce chaos and make it feel too hectic.

How are small shops seen in Tokyo? Small shops are very practical as real estate prices are ridiculous. Tokyo is very densely populated, and this is reflected in the way people live. People are very used to living, working, eating and shopping in a smaller space. Everything is adapted so it works in confined areas. For instance, the trains are absolutely packed like sardine cans, and the restaurants can be very small, yet full of people. As a result of this, your client often wants to shove as much product onto shelves as possible, and that is a great challenge for you as a retail designer because you want to do the opposite, and create something beautiful instead. So there always has to be a lot of compromise.

In 2008 Steve Lidbury closed his Tokyo practice to join London design practice TP Bennett.

opposite THE SIMPLE AND STRONG DESIGN MAKES THE ENTIRE SPACE VISIBLE FROM THE STREET.

below FLOOR PLAN OF THE STORE.

Timbuk2 had previously sold its messenger bags at specialist cycle or streetwear retailers, but decided it was time to have its own dedicated store. The idea was to create a space where the experience of the product and brand could be more tightly controlled, but it was also to function as a place where people could come to actually feel and select fabrics if they wanted to commission a customized bag. Touch is, of course, a sense not possible in the world of Internet shopping, and Timbuk2's website could now cheekily proclaim 'shopping at a store is the new shopping online'.

Naturally, Timbuk2 chose its hometown of San Francisco, where it also makes the bags, for its first store. A site was selected in the historic neighbourhood of Hayes Valley and the design entrusted to local architect William Duff. The budget was tight and the brief tricky, as the store had to remain true to the brand's street heritage within the small, enclosed environment of a boutique. Duff chose to keep things very simple.

For an urban flavour, a polished concrete floor was

162-165
TINY

TIMBUK2
San Francisco, California, USA
William Duff Architects
48m²/517ft²

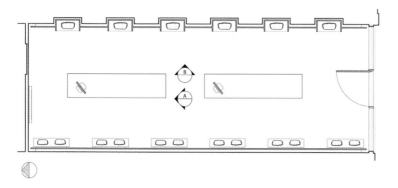

specified, and the entire back wall, with a concealed door to the rear storage area, is given over to a full-size graphic depicting the Timbuk2 logo in a way that suggested street art. Existing brickwork was painted rather than plastered over, and industrial-style light fittings installed, together with tables and signage using rugged metal. A conventional service counter was dispensed with, and in its place small, flat-screen computers were installed on the central tables.

Within this tough shell, two backlit display walls were simply floated down the sides of the space, allowing a straightforward and uncluttered presentation of the bags. All this is visible though a simple yet strong glass-and-steel storefront that maintains the urban, masculine feel of the place. Clarity and sense of purpose is what Duff is most proud of – qualities that are very much apparent here.

left MERCHANDISE IS DISPLAYED ON TWO WALLS FLOATED DOWN THE SIDES OF THE STORE. THE EXPOSED BRICKWORK BEHIND THEM IS SIMPLY PAINTED WHITE.

right BAGS ARE DISPLAYED ON ALTERNATING RAILS AND NICHES ON THE RIGHT SIDE OF THE STORE.

'THE STORE HAD TO REMAIN TRUE TO THE BRAND'S STREET HERITAGE.'

MATERIALS
- Metal tables
- Polished concrete floor
- Painted brick walls

SIS. DELI + CAFÉ

Helsinki, Finland
Muotohiomo
46m²/495ft²

SIS. DELI+CAFÉ

VESI	1,5 €
KIVENNÄISVESI	2,5 €
VIRVOITUSJUOMAT	2,5 €
TUOREMEHUT	3,5 €
SMOOTHIET	3,5 €
FUNKTIONAALISET JUOMAT	4,0 €
—	
KAHVI / NORMI	2,0 €
KAHVI / JÄTTI	2,5 €
TEE	2,0 €
ESPRESSO	1,5 €
TUPLAESPRESSO	2,5 €
LATTE	3,5 €
CAPPUCCINO	3,0 €
KAAKAO	3,0 €

opposite THE FEEL OF THE STORE IS SOFT AND RELAXED DESPITE THE BLACK-AND-WHITE COLOUR SCHEME.

left THE INTERIOR DESIGN TAKES ITS CUE FROM THE CHEQUERED BRANDING, HERE SEEN ON A CARRIER BAG.

'I WANTED SOMETHING AGELESS AND EASY-GOING BUT NOT RETRO.'

Sometimes, branding and packaging inspires an interior rather than the other way around. And SIS, a chain of health-food delicatessens and fast-food outlets in Finland, is a good example of this. The concept of the chain, from the bags to the whole retail environment, was developed as a unity by Helsinki design consultancy Muotohiomo, with a black-and-white Prince of Wales check extending subtly across everything from packaging to the awning outside. The name is a reference to their clients: two sisters called Anu Syrmä and Kaisa Leikola.

Given that the chain offers organic health foods, something of a novelty in Finland, the unified approach to the branding and interior had to create something that was 'easy going and relaxed', says Aleksi Perälä, in charge of interior design while then still at Muotohiomo. And it had to be the antithesis of McDonald's. 'We all hated over-branded concepts,' he says.

The basic idea was to create a modern Finnish equivalent of a traditional French *boulangerie*, but not a

MATERIALS
- 'Rocket' stools by Eero Aarnio, manufactured by Artek
- Wall illustrations by Klaus Haapaniemi
- White-waxed Finnish pine
- Custom shop fitting made from Durat

pastiche. 'I wanted the interior to be something ageless and easy-going but not retro and with a strong Finnish heritage,' he says. 'For me Finnish design means a combination of minimalist and functional design and a warm, human, friendly feeling. All that is created through use of materials, colours and shapes. And of course graphics.'

The branding and distinctive, confident graphics lent a pared-down, largely black-and-white colour scheme to the interiors, allowing the food products themselves to provide the colour highlights. Two materials were used for the bespoke shop furniture. One is soft black Durat, a recycled, polyester-based product. The other is local pine, which despite Finland's abundant forests has fallen out of fashion and which here was treated with white wax.

Black-and-white Rocket stools by Eero Aarnio are the only non-bespoke furniture items in the space. They were chosen, says Perälä, because their smooth edges were perfect for the cosy yet modern atmosphere he was working to achieve. Any metal in the store was given a painted finish, to blend with the 'soft' feel of the interior.

Muotohiomo's graphics-led approach is underscored by the illustrations that adorn the walls. These were commissioned from Klaus Haapaniemi, a well-known Finnish illustrator now resident in London. Relinquishing his usual colourful approach, Haapaniemi took Finnish children's tales as a starting point to create his black-and-white bears, lynxes and wolves.

opposite TWO FINNISH DESIGN STARS FEATURE IN THE STORE – ILLUSTRATOR KLAUS HAAPANIEMI CREATED THE ANIMAL DOOR DECORATIONS AND THE WELL-KNOWN ROCKET STOOLS WERE DESIGNED BY EERO AARNIO.

left EXAMPLES OF THE PREPARED FOOD AND ITS PACKAGING OFFERED BY SIS.

MAGMA PRODUCT STORE

London, UK
Nikki Blustin, Blustin Heath Design and Julie Blum, Inside Out
45m²/484ft²

left ALL THE FURNITURE IN THE STORE, INCLUDING THE COUNTER ON THE RIGHT, IS MADE FROM LAMINATED CARDBOARD.

below FLOOR PLAN. 1/COUNTER, 2/MODULAR FLAT-PACKED SHELVING UNITS WITH BACKLIGHTING, 3/FLOOR-TO-CEILING SHELVING.

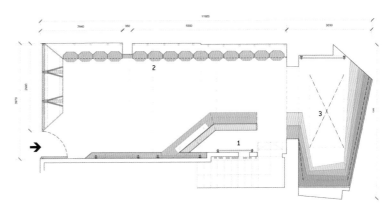

'Absolutely everything, from the counter to the shelving to the downstairs changing rooms, is made from cardboard.' So says Marc Valli, co-owner of the Magma Product Store in London's Covent Garden – the latest in a series of Magma stores in London catering to the city's designers and design-aware consumers. While the other London stores sell books and magazines and have a somewhat cultic following, this sells almost anything else: from T-shirts to cups and from jewellery to cameras. Just about any interestingly designed object qualifies.

Perhaps surprisingly, Shigeru Ban – the Japanese architect renowned for his cardboard structures – was not an inspiration. 'We were just kind of keen on the idea of cardboard,' says Valli. The material gives this store an intriguing feel, mixing the smooth sides of the cardboard panels with a honeycomb texture where it has been cut and stacked.

The store's design is the result of a collaboration between architects Nikki Blustin, of Blustin Heath Design,

right THE BACK-LIT DISPLAY UNITS ON THE LEFT-HAND SIDE OF THE STORE ARRIVED FLAT-PACKED.

below THE PATTERNS OF THE CUT CARDBOARD ACT AS AN EFFECTIVE FOIL TO THE MERCHANDISE, WHILE ALSO BEING DECORATIVE.

and Julie Blum, of Inside Out. Their plans were sent off to a structural packing company, which then carefully engineered the actual cardboard fittings for the shop, working out which folds would result in the shapes and strengths required. Environmental friendliness was a welcome bonus to the approach, and the company concerned, SCA Packaging, used pulp from their own managed forest in Sweden.

'The shop actually arrived flat-packed,' recalls Valli, and while it was all made to measure, there were some issues that needed ironing out. A wall had to be rebuilt as the bespoke fitting didn't fit, and the counter ended up being a full ten centimetres (four inches) higher than expected as they hadn't taken fully into account the way in which the folding would add to the height. 'No one had done anything like it; not in England anyway,' says Valli.

The last thing Valli wanted was a shop that looked precious and self-consciously 'designed'. 'We wanted it to be like Muji, but taken a step forward,' he says. 'We wanted it to be intelligent, but unpretentious and natural.

We didn't want to try and outdo the designers who come to our store – that would be pretentious. And we also didn't want it to seem high-end or expensive, just to look good and be original.'

While all the fittings in the Magma stores are bespoke, the budget for each was very limited. So, for the Product Store, the existing floor was retained, despite entreaties from the architects. 'We just removed the bubblegum,' jokes Valli. With the passage of time, the counter is showing signs of wear and exhibiting a slight bend, so it will probably be rebuilt with a wood frame. Lighting was an issue, and is an area where Valli thinks things could be improved. The shelves are backlit and ceiling-mounted spots take care of the rest.

'WE DIDN'T WANT TO TRY AND OUTDO THE
DESIGNERS WHO COME TO OUR STORE
— THAT WOULD BE PRETENTIOUS.

MATERIALS
• Bespoke corrugated
  cardboard display
  units

opposite THE INTIMATE ENCLOSED
DISPLAY AREA AT THE REAR OF THE
STORE.

left CARDBOARD ROLLS ARE USED TO
CREATE WALLS FOR THE STORAGE AREA
AND THE CHANGING ROOM DOWNSTAIRS.

SNEAKERS DELIGHT

Lisbon, Portugal
Igor Vidal Ferreira
40m²/431ft²

THE INTERIOR WALLS DECORATED BY
FRENCH ILLUSTRATOR SKWAK AWAITING
'COLOURING IN' BY VISITORS.

Sneakers Delight is a small shoe shop eking out a chameleon existence in Lisbon's fashionable Bairro Alto. It was the labour of love of Igor Ferreira. Lacking a formal design background, Ferreira nevertheless had the confidence and enthusiasm to create a small shop that became a destination in a way that established design consultancies and big brands find so difficult to achieve.

Every year, Ferreira had redecorated the space according to the stock and his own whim, before selling the shop in 2007 to a friend who is, however, retaining his services to design future iterations of the store. Ferreira's father worked in the theatre as a set-builder, providing invaluable technical assistance when needed, and some of the provisional and experiential nature of set-design seems to have rubbed off on the successive designs of the store.

'I think a shop should not only be a place where you go to buy your sneakers,' says Ferreira. 'It should be like an experience and not just buying and selling stuff. I think,

'I THINK A SHOP SHOULD NOT ONLY BE
A PLACE WHERE YOU GO TO BUY YOUR
SNEAKERS.'

although it can take attention away from the shoes, that it's more fun to have a shop where people come in and have more to look at than just the shoes (or whatever you are selling). It is also more fun for me this way.'

For the fourth and final redesign while he still owned Sneakers Delight, and to showcase the Adidas Originals range, Ferreira hit upon the idea of creating what he describes as 'an interactive decoration in black and white'. The surfaces were decorated in the busy and intricate children's book style of French illustrator Skwak, and marker pens were put at the disposal of shoppers, who were invited to 'colour in' the store.

Ferreira had originally seen the work of Skwak in a magazine. It impressed him enough to invite the illustrator over to Portugal from his base in Lille, northern France, to decorate the store.

opposite and above VISITORS TO THE STORE WERE ENCOURAGED TO USE MARKER PENS TO 'COLOUR IN' THE WALL DESIGNS.

right ADIDAS TRAINERS ARE SIMPLY LINED UP ALONG THE EDGE OF THE BLACK FLOOR IN THE VERY SIMPLE, YET EFFECTIVE, MERCHANDISING OF THE STORE.

THE STORE WAS TRANSFORMED INTO A RIOT OF COLOURS AFTER SHOPPERS AND VISITORS HAD DRAWN ON THE WALLS.

MATERIALS
• Bespoke colour-in wall decorations by illustrator Skwak

WATX

Barcelona, Spain
Martí Guixé
$35m^2/377ft^2$

WATX, a franchise selling different watch brands, has more than 30 stores throughout Spain, all designed to a common prescription by Catalan designer Martí Guixé. The shop illustrated in these pages is one of the nine WATX outlets in Barcelona, but any would do.

The WATX stores are a bold mix of regulated and haphazard. Mini retail environments – in the form of tightly controlled display cases for individual brands that are almost like little aquariums – are placed in what seems a very loosely conceived overall design, as if plonked down randomly in a factory outlet. Guixé refers to the box-shaped display cases as 'shops-in-the-box' with 'flexible micro-decoration'. The idea is to draw the shopper into the worlds of the different brands on offer, which include DKNY, Nike, Diesel, Dolce & Gabbana, and so on, and allow comparisons between each, or what Guixé calls 'zapping'.

Guixé's WATX is a deliberate challenge to the norms of retail design. It's more of a design system and concept

opposite THE CHALLENGE OF THESE
FRANCHISED STORES IS TO FIND A WAY
OF PRESENTING THE DIFFERING WATCH
BRANDS TOGETHER WITHOUT DILUTING
EACH BRAND.

right EACH OF THE STORES WAS
DESIGNED ACCORDING TO ONE OF THESE
INSTRUCTION CARDS, WHICH DETERMINE
MANY OF THE DESIGN PARAMETERS BUT
NOT FLOOR PLANS.

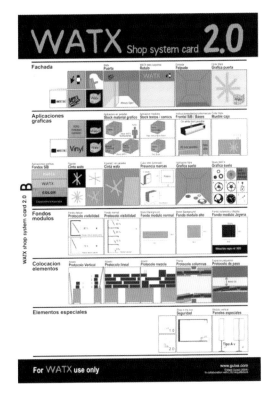

MATERIALS
• Aluminium and wenge
  wood display boxes
• Vinyl graphics
• Spotlighting

than a retail design in the conventional sense, and one
that takes the staples of a franchising system and gives
it a further nudge. Obviously, it is an approach that is not
oversensitive to size, other than that it can easily work in
very small spaces.

Guixé doesn't work in the usual way, from a floor
plan. Instead, the design of each of the stores is guided
by instruction cards, a recipe of sorts, with the design
department of WATX left to execute the actual interior
according to prescribed ingredients. As a consequence
of this design concept, Guixé is careful to call the project
a collaboration.

So how does Guixé feel the project has gone? 'In
the beginning, as usual, WATX were very insecure with
everything. But after a couple of years it started to work
very well (as a franchising system), and last year I added
some refinements to the system.'

On the subject of collaboration, Guixé's working
partnership with footwear brand Camper is one of the
most influential and highly regarded of joint retail efforts.

But WATX, due to its conceptual purity and prioritizing of
the functional over the formal, is perhaps closer to Guixé's
critical take on current design.

'THE DESIGN OF EACH OF THE STORES IS GUIDED BY INSTRUCTION CARDS.'

LULU PETITE

San Francisco, California, USA
CCS Architecture
35m²/377ft²

'NEARLY EVERY SURFACE, FROM DISPLAY UNIT TO MENU CLIPBOARD, IS YELLOW.'

Its very name announces the fact that it is going to be small. So small, in fact, that the display units of LuLu Petite, a delicatessen in San Francisco, are mobile, allowing them to be pushed out of the tiny shop and into the public area of the mall outside.

Located in San Francisco's historic Ferry Building, LuLu Petite was designed by Cass Calder Smith, now known as CCS Architecture. As it had been responsible for a Lulu restaurant (Restaurant LuLu) in the same city some ten years previously, it was natural for CCS to be brought in to design the restaurant's new little sister, LuLu Petite.

So that LuLu Petite could have a distinct identity among the many different stores in the revamped Ferry Building, CCS decided to adopt a clean and simple modernist approach and a distinctive colour scheme. Nearly every surface, from display unit to menu clipboard, is yellow, for which the architects specified yellow Finland plywood – or Finply. It is an approach that allows the simple, strong graphics (by Michael Mabry) to have maximum impact.

right THE STORE EXPANDS INTO THE PEDESTRIAN AREA OUTSIDE DURING OPENING HOURS.

below FLOOR PLAN. 1/PEDESTRIAN PASSAGE, 2/PREP KITCHEN, 3/GRAB-AND-GO REFRIGERATOR, 4/RETAIL SHELVES, 5/RETAIL AREA, 6/POINT OF SALE, 7/CUSTOMER SEATING.

This deli trades off its association with the LuLu restaurant, selling own-branded foods from the South of France. As well as its well-stocked shelves and gourmet deli-counter, LuLu Petite also has minimal seating for those who want to eat quickly on the premises.

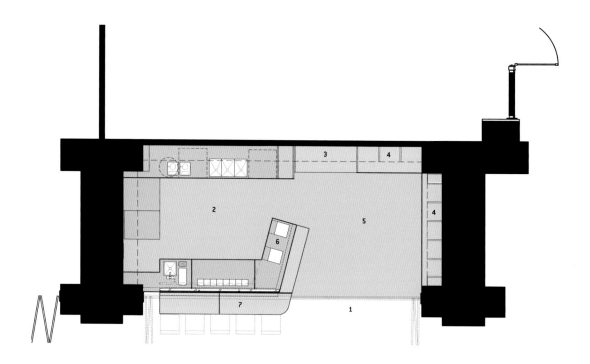

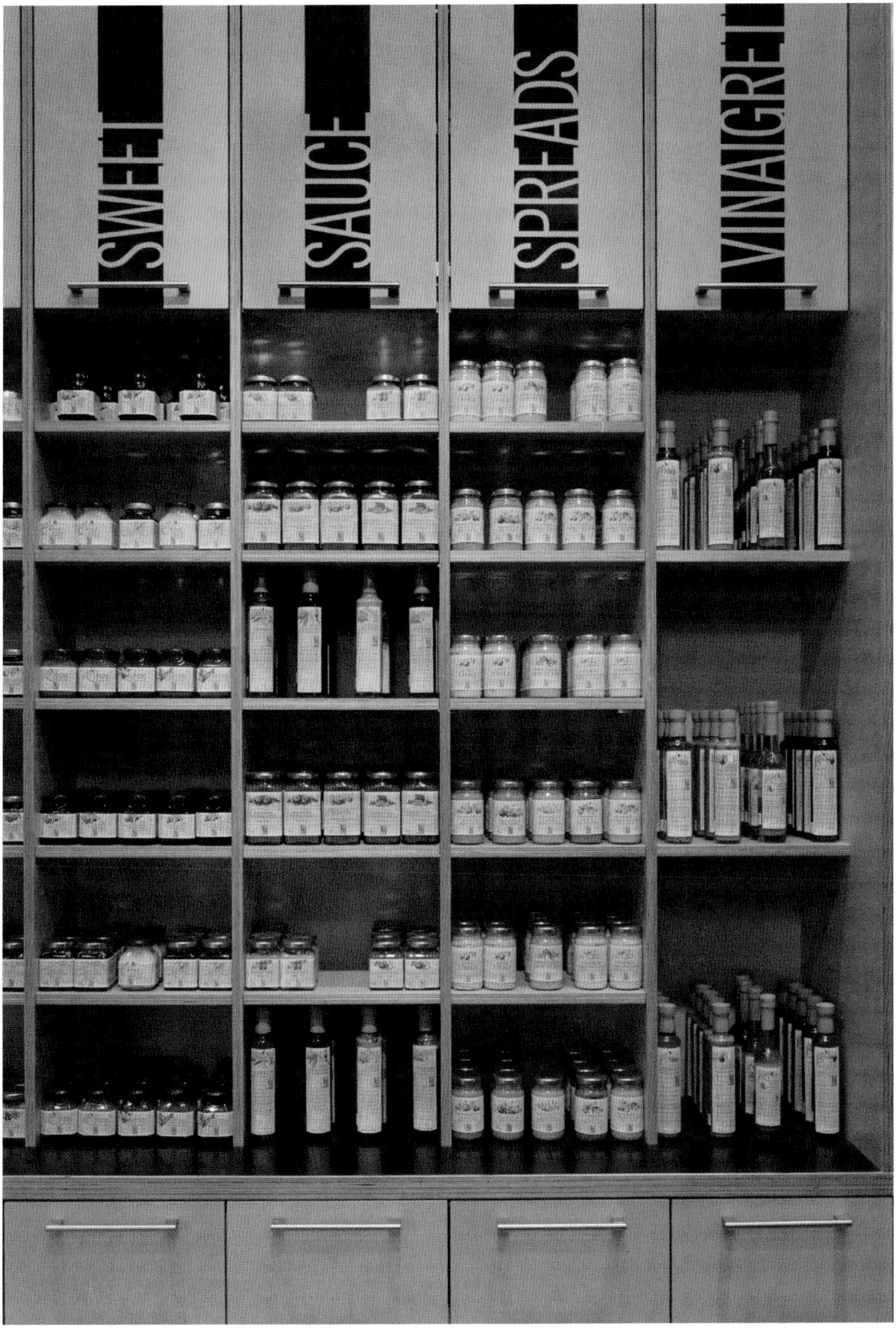

SWEET

SAUCE

SPREADS

VINAIGRE

SIMPLE AND STRONG GRAPHICS BY
MICHAEL MABRY ADORN THE YELLOW
PLYWOOD FITTINGS.

MATERIALS
• Plywood (Finply)
• Menus in the same
  material as shop
  furniture

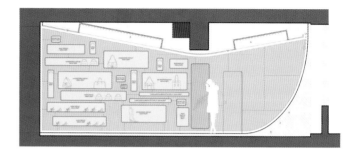

192-195
TINY

MARNI ACCESSORIES SHOP
Milan, Italy
Sybarite
30m²/323ft²

Few fashion brands have a retail design identity as immediately identifiable as Marni. Featured in countless glossy magazines, its trademark swooping clothes rail – which incorporates the clothing into the store design – was developed while Sybarite's founders Simon Mitchell and Torquil McIntosh were still at Future Systems. But the client followed the pair over to their new practice and they were entrusted with the continued roll-out of stores around the world.

The chain's success meant it was looking to establish a separate chain of accessory shops, with a new retail concept of its own. And again Sybarite was charged with developing the design, starting off with a small shop space that became available immediately in front of Marni's existing boutique on Via Della Spiga in Milan.

Ingeniously, the designers decided to manipulate the tight space with a 'pinched-in' design that uses enhanced perspective to add intrigue and drama. So, the walls and ceiling are compressed inwards for some two-thirds of the long stretch of floor, before widening out again.

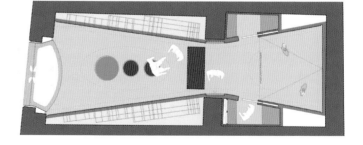

The area after the pinch contains fitting and storage rooms. These rooms aren't apparent when entering the shop — instead the eye is drawn to the converging, lacquered side walls into which irregular cubbyholes are cut to display the merchandise. Lined in a contrasting yellow, these are made of fibreglass and are backlit to make the merchandise as arresting as possible. The main lighting for the shop, however, comes from above, via two large, elliptical shapes that are cut into the ceiling but covered by stretched fabric to maintain the streamlined retro look.

Carpeted throughout in a soft grey, the floor curves up at the rear of the shop to join the wall. Mannequins emanate surreally from holes in this curved surface, as if from Swiss cheese, providing a display area and focal point at the furthest reach of the shop.

As with many small shops, a formal window display is discarded in favour of teasing potential shoppers by making the eye-catching interior as visible as possible. In this case, a simple and neutral steel-and-glass door

'MANNEQUINS EMANATE SURREALLY FROM HOLES, AS IF FROM SWISS CHEESE.'

acts as the entire frontage and window on to the inside.

The concept, combining retro and surreal elements, also has the benefit of being modular and adaptable for different footprints — essential as this is the blueprint for a global roll-out.

MATERIALS
- Grey carpet
- Lacquered walls
- Fibreglass display units
- Stretched fabric lighting covers

MYKITA

Berlin, Germany
Philipp Haffmans, Daniel Haffmans, Harald Gottschling and
Moritz Krüger
25m²/269ft²

opposite THE SIMPLE, ALL-WHITE DESIGN, REVOLVING AROUND TWO INTERLOCKED WALLS, IS CLEAR FROM THE STREET.

left FLOOR PLAN.

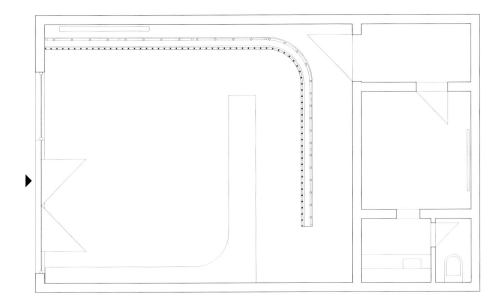

Philipp Haffmans and Harald Gottschling are designers of highly sought-after luxury eyewear under their own MYKITA brand. So, when they decided to have their own shop in Berlin, it needed, of course, to demonstrate the same attention to detail as their own glasses, which would be on sale with a handful of other brands.

Unusually, they decided to take on the entire task of designing the store themselves, drawing on the help of fellow founders Daniel Haffmans and Moritz Krüger, as well as others in the company. The only 'outside' design contribution came from Lars Grau, who conceived the ambitious lighting installation – something that required technical expertise that the in-house team didn't possess.

Located in a residential *Plattenbau* (concrete prefab) building on the Rosa-Luxemburg-Strasse, in an area of the city that had formerly been part of communist East Berlin, the site they chose had many advantages – not least an almost completely square space. 'The size didn't matter and we thought it would be a good spot to

represent the origin of our brand,' says Philipp Haffmans.

'The initial idea of the shop was to create an ideal platform for our frames,' he adds. 'We wanted it to be as simple and as smart as possible at the same time. The white walls and the bright light create a comfortable, yet cool, atmosphere.'

The design depends on two L-shaped walls that curve inwards as they approach the rear of the shop. The lower wall to the right, as it bends round, doubles as a sales counter. The higher wall on the left is used as a display rack. Both walls are an ethereal presence, with neon light programmed to pulsate through the many little holes puncturing their surface.

While these walls seem to be made of lace, they in fact feature an ingenious appropriation of the modular support rails used by the inexpensive, ubiquitous Dexion shelving system. Here, by being placed next to each other and given a shiny white powder-coated finish, the rails are transformed into something very different. However, their original function as a shelving support remains, and

'FORMER SWISSAIR SERVING TROLLEYS ARE PRESSED INTO SERVICE AS FLEXIBLE STORAGE.'

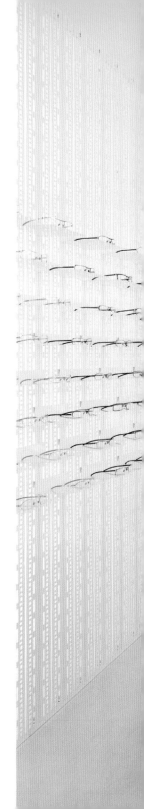

right SWISSAIR SERVING TROLLEYS ARE COVERED IN THE SAME SANDBLASTED BLEACHED ASH AS THE COUNTER SERVICE, CONTINUING THE ALL-WHITE DESIGN SCHEME.

overleaf DEXION SHELVING UNITS WERE PAINTED IN WHITE AND PLACED NEXT TO EACH OTHER TO CREATE AN ETHEREAL WALL AND DISPLAY SYSTEM.

tiny shelves carry various spectacle frames. A simple, all-glass shop frontage allows the appealing geometry of the display to be visible from outside the store.

Similar ingenuity is apparent in the use, or rather reuse, of former Swissair serving trolleys, now pressed into service as a flexible storage system that can also be used as a movable table in the store. As with everything in the shop, they too are white. Their tops, like that of the shop counter, are made of ash that is four centimetres (one-and-a-half inches) thick, sandblasted and then treated with lye to make them as pale as possible while offering a difference in texture.

Some of the lighting comes from spots placed simply overhead, but most comes from neon lights shining through fabric that has been positioned behind the 'lacy' walls. During the day the lighting is set to pulsate, but at night the whole space is transformed into a light installation. A programmed sequence is in play until a motion sensor in the shopfront detects passers-by, who are then treated to a light show that interacts with them.

All of this means that the front of the store becomes a lens on to a different world. A subtle message about the eyewear products on offer that is too subliminal for most to notice, this nevertheless gives the light installation enough relevance to stop it from being completely arbitrary.

MATERIALS
- Reused Swissair serving trolleys
- Dexion shelving units with white powder-coated finish
- Countertops of sandblasted ash bleached with lye

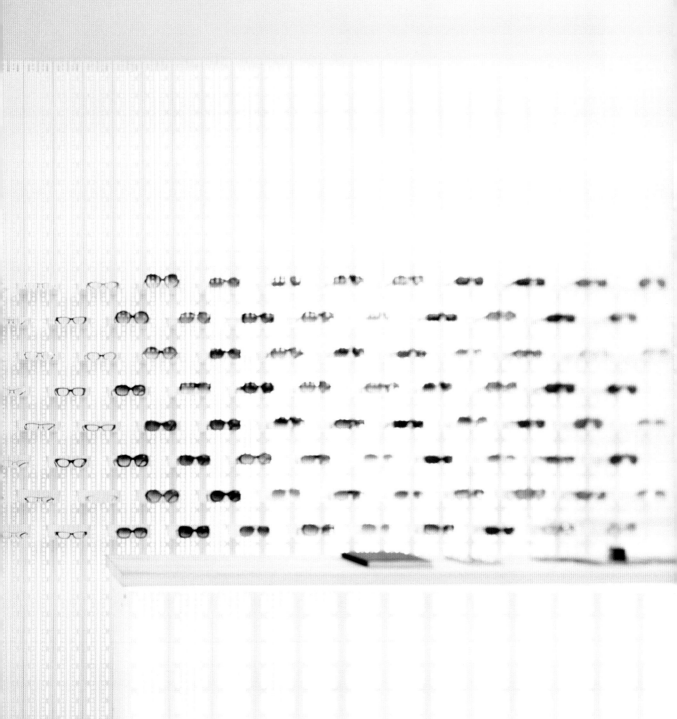

AZZEDINE ALAÏA SHOE SHOP

Paris, France
Designer: Marc Newson; Associate architect: Sébastien Segers
23m²/248ft²

Descending a flight of seven gentle steps deposits you at an altar to the shoe. A fetishist's delight, the tiny yet grand circular space is the shoe and accessory shop of Tunisian-born fashion designer Azzedine Alaïa.

The form of the shop is reminiscent of a Roman temple, an association underscored by the use of precious Carrara marble, here painstakingly crafted. Roman temple references are also echoed elsewhere: in the off-centre, marble-clad support column, which also functions as the base for a cushioned banquette; in the 12 niches cut into the marble walls, in which shoes and accessories are displayed; and in a circular ceiling lantern.

'The project is like a jewel case of white marble from Carrara, with its cylindrical shape concealing the original complex volume and it recreates pure, unique and concentric or dynamic space,' explains Sébastien Segers, who collaborated with Marc Newson on the project. 'We wanted to achieve a pure but complex design. We have worked with only three materials and simple lines, but simultaneously searched for sophisticated details.'

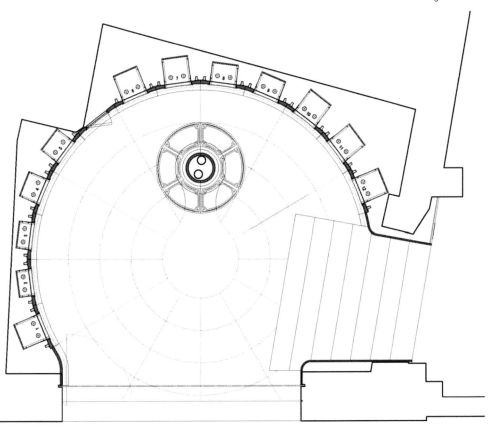

'ITS FORM IS REMINISCENT OF A ROMAN TEMPLE.'

Despite the luxurious materials, the shop is intended to function as a platform for the shoes. 'The seeming simplicity of the design leaves all the visual field to the Alaïa creations,' suggests Segers.

The three materials used are Carrara marble, brass and flesh-coloured calf leather, and they provide contrasts in texture, colour and temperature. The leather (used to line the niches and for the cushions on the banquette) is of a similar hue to the linings of the shoes on offer. A subliminal connection is made between the textural relationship of the soft calf leather and hard marble support, and that of the beautifully crafted shoe and the foot as it walks over hard surfaces.

The concentric pattern of the floor tiles is echoed by the recessed, circular brass light fitting. As with all of the shop's elements, this was meticulously custom-designed and manufactured. Some of the project's features were executed on-site by the designers themselves.

The shoe shop occupies an awkwardly shaped corner within the Paris headquarters of Azzedine Alaïa

— a fashion icon of the 1980s who, after a brief spell in obscurity, has staged a remarkable comeback. A-listers are once again photographed in his clothes and he has been able to buy back the label from Prada, which nevertheless continues to produce leatherwear and shoes under the Azzedine Alaïa name. As well as the shoe shop (or temple), the headquarters also contains Alaïa's own home, his atelier and showroom and his tiny, three-room, boutique hotel.

Belgian-born Segers established his own design office in Paris after leaving the studio of Marc Newson in 2003, but continues to collaborate with the Australian designer on a variety of interior projects.

left DETAIL OF THE LEATHER-LINED DISPLAY NICHES.

opposite FLESH-COLOURED LEATHER CUSHIONS MAKE THE MARBLE COLUMN A MORE COMFORTABLE SEATING AREA.

208-213
TINY

SHU

Valletta, Malta
Chris Briffa Architects
21m²/226ft²

The pale-stoned shops lining the steep, sixteenth-century streets of Malta's capital Valletta may have atmosphere by the bucketload, but they have little by way of space. So, what do you do when you want to have a shoe shop that can display 75 pairs of shoes, and store another 600 pairs, and yet only have a small store measuring 7 by 3 metres (23 by 10 feet)?

The brief for Shu (part of an independent local fashion chain in Malta, selling shoes and accessories from fashion brands such as Fornarina, Miss Sixty and Camper) had architect Chris Briffa and his team scratching their heads. They worked out that, if they couldn't expand horizontally to accommodate their client's requirements, then they could expand vertically by bringing the basement underneath the shop into the equation.

So, shop and basement were conjoined into a single space. This was filled with a disproportionately large staircase that would double up to fulfil most of the shop's requirements. 'From the early sketches a vertical design approach was adopted, where space was conceived

left TRADITIONAL WROUGHT-IRON CONCEALS THE EXTERNAL AIR-CONDITIONING UNITS WHILE THE STAIRS DOUBLE AS A WINDOW DISPLAY FOR SHOES.

opposite CONCEPT SKETCH SHOWING THE OVERSIZED STAIRCASE AND USE OF THE BASEMENT SPACE.

MATERIALS
- African hardwood stairs
- 'Genoa' wallpaper by Osborne & Little
- Bespoke wrought-iron railings

above THE VERTIGINOUS VIEW DOWN THE STAIRS TO THE BASEMENT.

opposite THREE SECTIONAL DRAWINGS AND A MODEL SHOWING THE INTERLOCKING STAIRCASES THAT INGENIOUSLY MAXIMIZE SPACE AND DISPLAY AREA IN THE TINY STORE.

overleaf THE USE OF BLACK MIRRORS ADDS ANOTHER LAYER TO THE COMPLEX SPATIAL GAMES PLAYED BY THE STORE.

purely as access and consequently fragmented into one giant staircase combining display, seating, storage and all services into one element,' says Briffa. 'We imagined clients walking up, down and around the stairs, picking their favourite shoe, sitting next to it and trying it on.'

The design essentially revolves around three interlocking staircases. The result is a stepped space that shoppers are invited to explore, having different experiences as they go. In the process they become part of the display, replacing the standard shoe-shop window with something altogether more unusual and eye catching.

While such use of space might seem radical and surreal, this is counterbalanced by a feature that is playfully traditional and deferential to the island's heritage. Decorative white-painted, wrought-iron railings accompany the wooden steps as well as providing a balcony over the shopfront. Richly patterned damask wallpaper on the side walls softens the space and stops it from being too austere.

A visitor to the shop's opening observed to Briffa that the shop suggested Japanese 'shoebox' architecture held together by traditional Maltese ornament. While perhaps requiring shoppers who are especially agile and adventurous, the shop's ingenuity is undeniable. And all to a budget of 70,000 Euros ($109,000) and a four-month build.

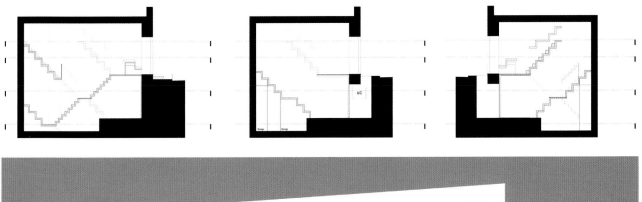

LARA BOHINC

London, UK
Mika Cimolini, Elastik
20m²/215ft²

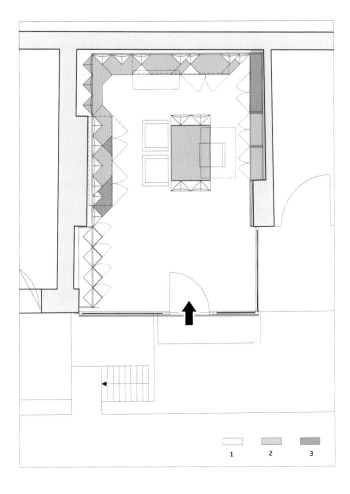

opposite THE RELATIVELY CONVENTIONAL EXTERIOR, TYPICAL FOR CHELSEA, GIVES LITTLE AWAY ABOUT THE DRAMA THAT LIES INSIDE.

left FLOOR PLAN. 1/DISPLAYS, 2/ SHELVES, 3/STORAGE AREAS.

1   2   3

'THE DARK, VAULT-LIKE ATMOSPHERE IS UNUSUAL FOR SUCH A SMALL SHOP.'

This shop is the outcome of the meeting of two friends. Mika Cimolini had gone to school with Lara Bohinc back home in Slovenia. Cimolini went on to study architecture in the Netherlands, and Bohinc to study jewellery design in London, but when their paths crossed again Bohinc asked her old friend to design a temporary shop in Hoxton, London, in 2002. And then, a few years on, came the commission to design a store in Chelsea.

'To work for another designer is always a challenge but it is also easier because designers are much more explicit about what they want,' says Cimolini, a founder of the architectural practice Elastik, which is based in both Slovenia and the Netherlands. 'We got a very clear project brief from Lara, with a lot of references such as "treasure box, Egyptian tomb, beehive..." and how she wanted the shop to be appealing for her clients, how the items should be placed on the shelves, and so on.'

Cimolini came up with a design that continued where the previous store left off and which would draw on

these new suggested references 'to create a specific story for Lara Bohinc'. The first, temporary, shop used textile membranes stretched over the space to dress and 'dematerialize' the walls, as well as generating a geometric rhythm. While this created an ethereal white space, the second shop preserves the sense of geometric play but adopts a very different structure – heavy, black and moulded – that functions both as decoration and shelving and is set off by a gold-coloured carpet.

The dark, vault-like atmosphere is unusual for such a small shop but was at Bohinc's suggestion. The result is luxurious and vaguely reminiscent of ancient treasure troves. Above all, it allows Bohinc's jewellery to take centre stage.

The modular structure that is the design's central conceit is also a deferential nod in the direction of the sculptural walls created by Austrian-born sculptor Erwin Hauer in the US during the 1950s and 60s. But, instead of stone, Elastik decided to use vacuum-pressed Kerrock, a composite acrylic-based material that has the feel

MATERIALS
• Gold coloured carpet
• Bespoke shelving
  made of Kerrock

of stone but can be shaped like wood. These modular elements are repeated through the store and contain the lighting elements, fixed so that no distracting shadows are cast across the space or break the spell. Their geometric regularity creates a background structure to support the jewellery in a rich yet subtle way.

The shop's exterior is a restored Victorian shopfront typical of this part of London. Such a conventional and conservative façade deliberately gives little warning of what lies inside.

HAPPY PILLS

Barcelona, Spain
M-M
20m²/215ft²

Composición:

100% ✚ happy pills

3% Azul cielo
5% Amarillo limon
2% Chiste verde
4% Humor negro
7% Carcajada descontrolada
8% La vie en rose
2% Cosquillas
7% Naranjas de la China
1% Fino humor British
2% Retranca gallega
6% Acento andaluz
9% Gol en el ultimo minuto
2% Esencia de amanecer
7% Ho ho ho
3% Algodón de Azúcar
2% Agujetas de reírse
5% Con faldas y a lo loco
4% Río de Janeiro
3% Tijuana
7% Excipiente de John Cleese
6% Ramo de margaritas
5% Siesta del Mediterráneo.

When M-M, a local design consultancy made up of four women with backgrounds in print, advertising and architecture, was approached to design and develop a concept for a sweetshop on Carrer dels Arcs, close to Barcelona's cathedral, they immediately noted two things: the space was tiny and there were no passing children to sell to.

Drawing on their experience in branding and advertising, M-M therefore decided to start from the product and worked outwards. 'If we couldn't sell sweets to children we would have to sell them to whoever walked by: adult Barcelona residents and tourists. For this we needed to make the sweets interesting for adults. We came up with the fact, more or less proven by all, that eating something sweet entails a slight improvement in mood,' says Marion Dönneweg.

So the concept of Happy Pills was born, and a faux pharmaceutical look was developed, not just for the design of the 'drug store' but also for its branding and packaging. As there was no budget to develop bespoke packaging, the designers co-opted plastic containers made for vitamins and other pills, some complete with their safety screw tops. Labels with 'instructions for use' are stuck to the containers according to the customer's chosen sweets, and are available in Spanish, English or Japanese. Some ready-made sweet selections are available, such as the 'First Aid Kits', but shoppers largely prefer to create their own.

The store itself was more of a problem, squeezed as it is between two much larger buildings. 'The design of the shop was complicated because it is very small and extremely narrow,' says Dönneweg. 'That created a difficulty for the circulation of customers inside the shop. We had to organize all the boxes with sweeties and everything else on one side, while the other side remains empty except for the graphics or "ingredients list". And the floor is metallic, using irregular pieces to hide the fact that the two walls aren't exactly parallel.'

The 'ingredients list' mentioned by Dönneweg is a huge menu of vital happiness ingredients stuck up on one wall of the corridor-like space. It includes such vital components as 'black humour', 'tickling', 'blue joke' and 'extract of John Cleese'. The actual sweets are dispensed and packaged in a bespoke, backlit acrylic structure on the other side of the corridor. The store's fascia, white walls and bright, 'clinical' lighting provide further humorous references to pharmacies and the world of medicine.

Consumers have overwhelmingly got the joke, and the concept has proved successful enough for the store's owner to have been approached regarding franchising the design internationally.

opposite BESPOKE ACRYLIC DISPENSERS
ARE FILLED WITH SWEETS FOR THOSE
WHO WANT TO MAKE THEIR OWN
SELECTION, WHILE THE LAZY CAN SELECT
FROM PRE-SELECTED KITS ABOVE.

right THE DISPLAY ON ONE SIDE OF THE
VERY NARROW SPACE FLOATS ABOVE A
METAL FLOOR, CAREFULLY CONSTRUCTED
TO MASK THE IRREGULARITIES OF
THE SITE.

'THE WHITE WALLS AND BRIGHT, CLINICAL LIGHT HUMOROUSLY REFER TO PHARMACIES AND CONSUMERS HAVE OVERWHELMINGLY GOT THE JOKE.'

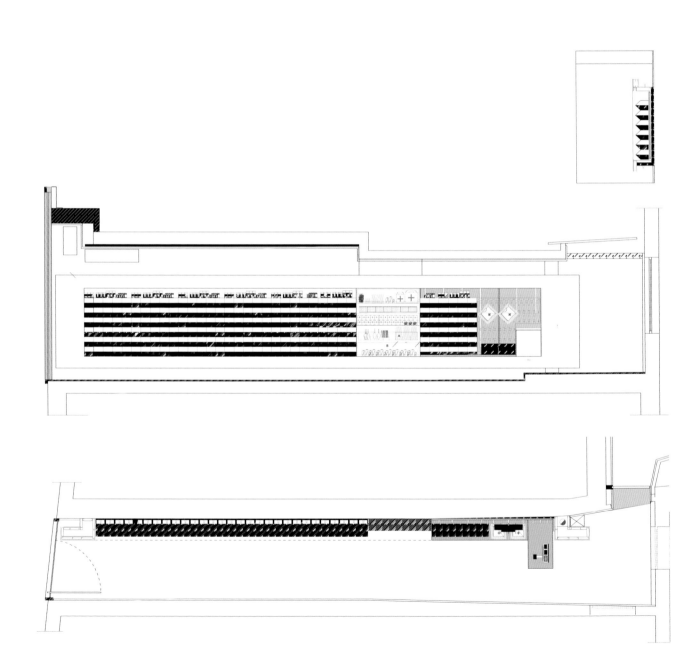

opposite FROM TOP: SECTION;
ELEVATION; FLOOR PLAN.

below THE PACKAGING CONTINUES THE
PHARMACEUTICAL JOKE, HERE GIVING
'INSTRUCTIONS' FOR TAKING THE SWEETS.

'I WANTED PEOPLE NOT TO KNOW WHERE THEY ARE OR HAVE ANY SENSE OF TIME.'

226-231

TINY

LADURÉE

Monte Carlo, Monaco
Roxane Rodriguez
20m²/215ft²

'I had *Alice in Wonderland* in my mind when I designed this store,' says Roxane Rodriguez. 'I wanted to create a little temple to *gourmandise* [gluttony].'

It was the latest in a series of magical interiors for Ladurée, the French company that has elevated the simple macaroon to the level of fetish. Anything that would specifically date the store, such as lighting or the till, is recessed from view, and the impression given is that the store has been just as it is for centuries. 'I wanted people not to know where they are or have any sense of time,' says Rodriguez. 'I wanted them to feel they are in a dream world.'

A trip to a local flea market in Paris yielded the chandelier – restored and painted gold in colour – that now hangs in the centre of the store. But the creation of this fairy-tale world also required some interesting (and very lavish) use of materials. The ethereal-looking floor has a curiously disconcerting geometry that was created by a resin layer covering some sprayed platinum. The surrounding black cabinets and brown ceiling were

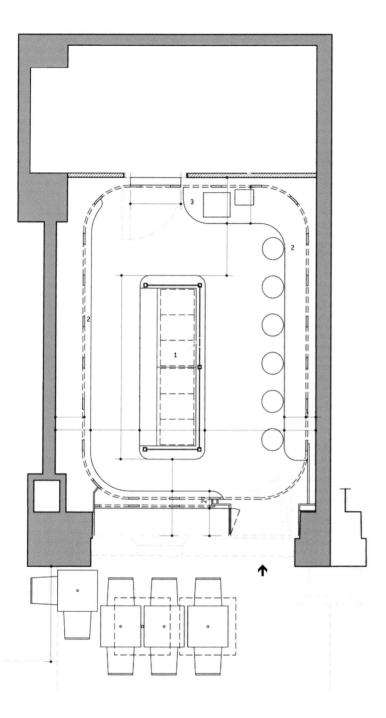

opposite A DUSTING OF SILVER AND GOLD MAKES THE BLACK LACQUERED DISPLAY UNITS SHIMMER IN THE LIGHT OF INTEGRATED LEDS.

left FLOOR PLAN. 1/MAIN MARBLE DISPLAY TABLE, 2/PERIMETER SHELVING, 3/HIDDEN CASH TILL.

lacquered as if they were little Japanese boxes, and a dusting of silver and gold allows them to shimmer in the light.

Apart from the central chandelier, lighting is provided by integrated trichromatic LEDs. These permit the mood in the shop to be varied during the day and night, without having any specific light fixtures to distract from the overall magical effect.

The counter, hewn from white marble, appropriately dominates the space, but its intricate carving prevents it from being too heavy and monumental a presence for the fairy-tale mood. Macaroons, chocolates and the other delicacies for sale are simply presented on trays on this counter.

DESPITE ITS SIZE, THE IMPOSING MARBLE
COUNTER SEEMS TO FLOAT – A RESULT
OF PLAYFUL DESIGN AND CAREFUL
LIGHTING.

MATERIALS
- Carved white marble counter
- Resin-covered platinum floor
- Gold and silver-sprayed black lacquer cabinets
- Chandelier from flea market
- Integrated LED lighting

MOBILE JOKER STORE

Hamburg, Germany
Spine Architects
$19m^2/205ft^2$

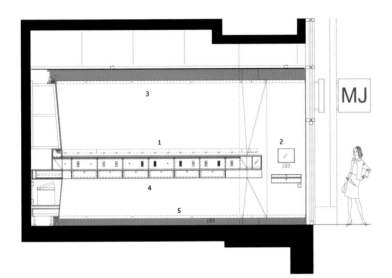

MJ

A narrow glass band winds its way around the tiny Mobile Joker Store's walls, jutting out slightly from a cabinet that seems to hover in space. Behind the glass is a selection of high-end mobile phones and other small electronic devices, presented almost as jewels or as objects that have been curated.

The overall effect of this Hamburg store is achieved by gently angling the walls back from the display, and then backlighting them from gaps between the ceiling and curved floor. A fastidious attention to detail means that nothing is allowed to interrupt the ribbon of display – for example, the storage drawers beneath the glass are flush to the display unit and almost imperceptible.

Likewise, the counter simply emanates organically from the wall to minimize any disruption to the shopper's experience of the strip of merchandise, teasingly presented to encourage a journey around the shop's perimeter. An irregular floor plan injects dynamism into the interior, and the widening of space towards the rear works to draw shoppers in.

MATERIALS
- Wall covered in laminated wood-based panels and painted plasterboard
- Epoxy-coated flooring
- Painted plasterboard ceiling

'NOTHING IS ALLOWED TO INTERRUPT THE RIBBON OF DISPLAY.'

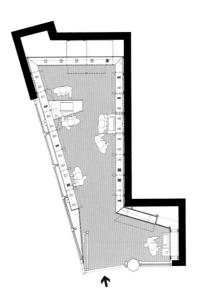

left THE DISPLAY UNITS – CONCEALING PUSH-LOADING DRAWERS AND STORAGE UNITS – SEEM TO FLOAT AS A RESULT OF BEING BACKLIT.

above FLOOR PLAN.

Dramatic lighting, and a first impression that suggests the unlikely combination of museum and club, allows this store to make an appropriate statement about the objects on sale. It is a conspicuously pure experience calculated to elevate and underscore the design ambitions of the expensive mobile phones on offer here.

Spine Architects, also based in Hamburg, is a relatively young outfit set up by architects who had worked at the practices of Jan Störmer, Will Alsop and Daniel Libeskind. Project architects Susanne Buckler and J'orn Hadzik clearly revelled in this commission to refurbish an existing tiny space, referring to the project internally as XSS.

The client, Etronixx Trading, conducts its business primarily online under the Mobile Joker brand, but also wanted a physical presence. What it got was a dramatic and refined pint-sized retail experience impossible to achieve with a website.

A PIECE OF CAKE

Zagreb, Croatia
Ivana Franke and Petar Mišković
18m²/194ft²

opposite THE CREATORS OF THE PASTRY STORE CONCEIVED IT AS AN 'EMPTY FRAME' THAT RELIES ON FORCED PERSPECTIVE AS ITS ONLY DECORATION.

right FLOOR PLAN SHOWING THE STORE'S FUNNEL-LIKE FALSE WALLS.

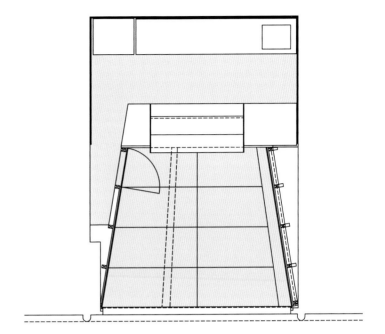

Trotting through shopping malls is all too often an experience of mindless banality. Walk through the Importanne Galleria in the Croatian capital Zagreb, however, and amid the identikit franchises you will come across an intriguing, indeterminate white space.

It turns out to be a pastry shop, with the suitably playful name of A Piece of Cake. And if it seems more like a conceptual work of art than a shop, that is no coincidence: the design was conceived by installation artist Ivana Franke and fellow Croatian Petar Mišković, a freelance architect.

The two had collaborated on the Croatian Pavilion for the Venice Biennale, and decided to work together on this project from the very first sketch. 'It was not Ivana's role to apply art after the architect's work was done,' explains Mišković. 'In her art objects – ambient and site-specific installations – she is usually dealing with space, light and perception, which makes her a precious partner.'

Up the road from Venice is the town of Vicenza, home of Renaissance architect Andrea Palladio and his Teatro

MATERIALS
- Floor, walls and ceiling of white-painted OSB (oriented strand board)
- Rear and display area walls covered with polycarbonate sheets
- Standard professional stainless-steel display counter, refrigerator and sink
- Recessed fluorescent tube lighting

Olimpico, or Olympic theatre. The radical perspectival foreshortening of this theatre's stage setting (actually by Vincenzo Scamozzi) influenced the pair's strategy for designing the pastry shop. Not only does their approach invite the curious shopper, but it makes the space seem bigger. 'We designed it as a preconstructed perspectival image of the space, so that it looks deeper than it actually is,' explains Mišković. 'We wanted it to look like an emptied frame rather than a generic shopping mall filling.'

The shape of the space is that of a funnel: floor, ceiling and side walls all converge. The perspectival play becomes one of the only forms of 'decoration' in the shop. And by taking out detail and converging the sides, the space seems bigger – an impression heightened by the dark end wall, which increases the sense of recession. The floor-level branding participates in the perspectival games, and when the trick 'stage door' (which gives access to the counter) opens, the magnitude of the spatial manipulation becomes evident.

The client wanted a shop that was primarily for selling pastries produced off-site, but a counter was installed should impatient or hungry shoppers want to eat their cake then and there. And, naturally, even this counter is part of the spatial trickery – it is actually level, but the ascending floor means that it is at different heights depending on where you are standing.

PIECE OF CAKE

opposite A CONCEALED DOOR GIVES ACCESS TO THE COUNTER AND CONCEALED WORKSPACE.

above NOT ONLY DO THE WALLS CONVERGE, BUT THE FLOOR RISES, TO CREATE PERSPECTIVAL TRICKS.

'WHEN THE TRICK "STAGE DOOR" OPENS, THE MAGNITUDE OF THE SPATIAL MANIPULATION BECOMES EVIDENT.'

PEYTON AND BYRNE AT HEAL'S

London, UK
FAT
18m²/194ft²

'THE PASTEL COLOURS OF TRADITIONALLY ICED CAKES INSPIRED SOME OF THE DETAILING.'

opposite THE STORE AIMS TO BE AN ARCHETYPAL CAKE SHOP THAT IS TRADITIONAL YET WITH AN UNEXPECTED TWIST.

below SKETCH SHOWING LAYOUT OF THE COUNTER AND SHELVES.

Heal's has long been the home furnishing store that typifies restrained modern British design. Tucked away in a small space at its entrance, where a florist once resided, is a small takeaway bakery called Peyton and Byrne. At first glance, it looks as though it must always have been here, in this famous Arts and Crafts-influenced building. But, on closer inspection, cheeky details such as a vibrant, crazily coloured glass mosaic floor give the game away.

The store is the brainchild of restaurateur Oliver Peyton, who wanted to create something that was the opposite of Starbucks. The idea was to offer old-school neglected British favourites such as Bakewell tart and Victoria sponge cake – things that your grandmother might like. Colourfully arranged, these cakes were to be rescued from unfashionable oblivion to become the stars of the show, along with supporting roles for other traditional fare such as pies and sausage rolls.

If Peyton's approach gave us British baking with a modern twist, the design of the diminutive store followed a similar recipe. Apart from chef Roger Pizey, responsible for the pastel-coloured, children's storybook cakes and tarts, Peyton enlisted the quirky yet very British talents of graphic designer Mark Farrow, and architects FAT, or Fashion Architecture Taste.

FAT say they wanted to create an archetypal store, and from the first glance through the heavy bronze window, it does indeed seem to be something brought to life from a children's book. The main decoration comes in the form of the cakes themselves, and the similarly enticing packaging by Farrow Design. While the store's design acts in a supporting role, it adds plenty of humour, making sure that the traditional references are fun rather than frumpy. 'A subtle, slightly oblique reference to Victorian and Edwardian shops' is how FAT's Charles Holland sums up the design.

The pastel colours of traditionally iced cakes inspired some of the detailing. While white brick tiling suggests a nineteenth-century store, the grouting is green. And the mosaic floor (designed on computer but put together by

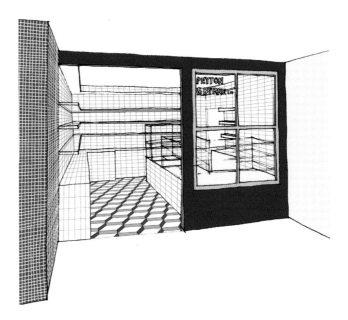

mosaic specialist Paul Marks) intersperses pistachio and candy pink with the traditional black and white, all in a busy Op Art-inspired, and off-centred, pattern.

Despite these touches, Holland says the restricted space meant that the bakery is not as decorative or narrative as the practice's work usually is. 'It couldn't be too ornate,' he says. 'We had to leave room for the cakes to sell themselves.' The main task, Holland says, was to keep things simple and not allow modern technologies, such as chiller cabinets, to intrude too much.

Simple glass shelving and tiled display surfaces could be Victorian, but then a cluster of reflector bulbs are grouped together to form an impromptu chandelier above. It's a playful engagement with traditional forms that manages not to be predictable or stodgily retro – an approach that also typifies Meals, the restaurant that FAT designed for Peyton inside Heal's itself.

MATERIALS
- Spotlight reflector bulbs grouped together for central light feature
- Green grouting
- White tiles
- Bronze window frame
- Glass mosaic floor

WELLIE WAGON

New York, New York, USA
TEAMcreative
*c.*4m^2/43ft^2

'WOODEN CUBBYHOLES WERE DESIGNED TO ECHO THE SHAPE OF THE SWEDISH FLAG.'

opposite THIS MOBILE WOODEN SHOP WAS ATTACHED TO A TRICYCLE, OFFERING WELLIES AND SHOES TO SHOPPERS ON THE STREETS OF NEW YORK.

overleaf A FOLDING BENCH AT THE REAR ALLOWED PEOPLE TO TRY ON THE SHOES IN COMFORT.

Of course, there is no law saying a store has to be static. Make it small enough and you can put wheels on it, and even put a tricycle up front. And that is precisely what Tretorn, the Swedish casual footwear brand owned by Puma, decided to do.

The 'Wellie Wagon', replete with a canvas rain canopy and cyclist-cum-shop-assistant at the helm, gently trundled the streets of New York in April 2008. It was offering people on the street the chance to buy Tretorn footwear – primarily galoshes – in much the same way as they might buy a hot dog.

Initially the idea of Antonio Bertone, Tretorn's chief marketing officer, this diminutive mobile shop was designed and fabricated by TEAMcreative, made up of husband and wife Tyler Evans and Alessandra Mondolfi, in 270 intensive hours over a three-week period. Lightweight 4130 Cromoly steel tubing and white oak plywood were used for the trailer-shop. The wooden cubbyholes that housed the shoes were designed to echo the shape of the Swedish flag and the Tretorn logo, a reference reinforced by the combination of blue canvas, yellowish wood and yellow-painted tricycle.

The trailer's tailgate folded down to provide a seating area for people wishing to try on the shoes. To make the cyclist's life easier, the tricycle has three gears and three brakes. While no doubt a marketing gimmick, the Wellie Wagon's tight design does suggest other avenues for retail design on a minute scale.

Imagine a tiny store that entices you with branded merchandise, but then puts it all unobtainably out of reach. A shop where you can only look and not buy. Maverick Parisian artist/designer and Tokyo resident Cyril Duval – who operates under the brand 'Item Idem' – creates installations and interventions using the world of retail as a playground. Nowhere is this more successfully expressed than in the Wrong Store.

Lovingly mocking the language of store design, the Wrong Store presented itself as '22m² × 3m³ [237ft² × 106ft³] of retail excitement' where, on weekends, there was a '50% more' sale. However, this little window on retail existed for just one month, during 2006. It was, in fact, created as part of an exhibition for the Galerie Frédéric Giroux in Paris, and takes the 'guerrilla store' concept pioneered by Comme des Garçons to its very limit.

Duval formally describes The Wrong Store as follows: 'A play on the modern fascination for retail culture; the desirable window image of a shop where no one can really enter and buy unless the purchase becomes the

248-249

TINY

THE WRONG STORE
Paris, France
Item Idem
c.1.5m²/16ft²

entire shop; a finalized retail *Gesamtkunstwerk* [total work of art] arising from adding together the concept, the architecture, and all associated artworks and products.'

It was inspired by conceptual artist Maurizio Cattelan's Wrong Gallery, a tiny exhibition space that moved around the world without ever really opening. This, says Duval, is its 'unauthorized and derivative souvenir shop'. It was also the first in an ongoing series of collaborations with Tobias Wong, who opened a similar Wrong Store of unbuyable objects in New York.

But, while playfully taking on the tropes of retail, Duval's Wrong Store is also a beautiful demonstration in itself of how engaging small shops can be. Having collaborated with Comme des Garçons and Collette, Duval's work is as much a celebration as a critique of the stances and spaces of small shops.

'A DESIRABLE WINDOW IMAGE OF A SHOP WHERE NO ONE CAN REALLY ENTER.'

SALE
OFF
WARHOL
GIFT WRAP
by Tobias Wong
ONLY
500 € - 1500 €
WILL RETURN

ARANAZ BOUTIQUE

2nd Floor, Greenbelt 5
Makati Avenue corner De La
Rosa Street
Makati City
1223 Philippines
www.aminava.blogspot.com
Design Juan Carlo Calma
www.juancarlocalma.com
Contractor Multi Development
and Construction Corporation
1125 Antipolo Street
Makati City
1223 Philippines

AZZEDINE ALAÏA SHOE SHOP

5 rue de Moussy
75004 Paris
France
Design Marc Newson
www.marc-newson.com
in association with Sébastien
Segers
www.sebastiansegers.com
Marble Furrer SPA, Carrara,
Italy
Saddlery Domeau & Peres
SARL, La Garenne Colombes,
France
Plasterworks SOE Stuc & Staff
SCOP, Paris, France
Metal works TPU SARL,
Chelles, France
Lighting Intension SARL,
Paris, France

CAMPER

6 via Monte Napoleone
20121 Milan
Italy
www.camper.es
Design Jaime Hayón in
association with Studio
Camper
www.hayonstudio.com

CHARLES FISH

320 Cabot Square East
London E14 4QT
UK
www.charlesfish.co.uk
Design Branson Coates
www.bransoncoates.com
Brand consultants Walford
Wilkie
www.w-wco.com

CONCEPTS

11A Brattle Street
Cambridge, MA 02138
USA
www.cncpts.com
Design: Soldier Design
www.soldierdesign.com
Client Tarek Hassan

CONTRAPUNTO

El Rodeo 12.850
Shopping La Dehesa, Local 14
Lo Barnechea, Santiago
Chile
**Architecture and furniture
design** Lipthay + Cohn +
Contenla
www.lc2.cl
Collaborators Diego Salinas
and Carolina Agliati
Constructor KIT CORP S.A.

EKO

288 Queen Street West
Toronto, Ontario M5V 2A1
Canada
www.EKOjewellery.com
Bennett C. Lo, Dialogue 38
www.dialogue38.com

ELSA BIJOUX

Calle Piamonte 8
28004 Madrid
Spain
Design Teresa Sapey Estudio
de Arquitectura
www.teresasapey.com
Graphic design Alex Gutwil
Project assistance Antje
Stuchlik, Angela Sanz

EMPEROR MOTH

93 Mount Street
London W1K 2S
UK
Design Ab Rogers Design
www.abrogers.com
In collaboration with D. A.
Studio and Dominic Robson
(BLINK!)
www.blinkdesign.com
Shop fitting Harry Van Rooij

F-SHOP

Klosterwall #9
D-20095 Hamburg
Germany
www.freitag.ch
Architecture blauraum
www.blauraum.de
Client FREITAG Lab
www.freitag.ch

GEOMETRY

Gipsstraße 23
10119 Berlin Mitte
Germany
www.geometrytheshop.de
Design Plajer & Franz Studio
www.plajer-franz.de
Graphics and signage Studio
38
www.studio38.de

HAPPY PILLS

Carrer dels Arcs 6
Barcelona
Spain
**Product concept, creative
strategy, brand and store
design** Marion Dönneweg,
Mireia Roda, Merche Alcalá
Copywriter Jorge Virgós
Production Maria Tarrés
www.m-m.es

HOLTS LAPIDARY
98 Hatton Garden
London EC1N 8NX
UK
www.holtsgems.com
Architecture Blauel Architects
www.blauel.com
Brand consultants Walford
Wilkie
www.w-wco.com

HUNT & GATHER
225 Carrall St.
Vancouver, British Columbia
V6B 2J2
Canada
www.huntandgather.ca

**JIN'S GLOBAL
STANDARD**
Nagareyamaotakanomori
SC 2F
6-185-2 Nishihatsuishi
Nagareyama-shi, Chiba
Japan
Design Ryuji Nakamura
Architects. Co., Ltd.
www.ryujinakamura.com

LADURÉE
Europa Résidence
Place des Moulins
98000 Monte Carlo
Monaco
www.laduree.com
Design Agence Roxane
Rodriguez
18 Rue de Seine
75006 Paris
France

LARA BOHINC
149F Sloane Street
London SW1X 9BX
UK
Design Mika Cimolini, Igor
Kebel with assistance of
Tomaz Pipan and Grega Pilih
– Elastik
www.elastik.net
Lighting design Soncesenca
Carpentry Domiles d.o.o.,
Ljubljana
Refurbishment AGH d.o.o.,
Ljubljana

LE LABO
233 Elizabeth Street
New York, NY 10012
USA
www.lelabofragrances.com
Eddie Roschi and Fabrice
Penot, Le Labo, with Auric
Consultancy + Design
www.auricprojects.com

LIL SHOP
Brunnenstrasse 184
D-10119 Berlin Mitte
Germany
www.lil-shop.com
Design Lil Schlichting-
Stegemann

LINDEN APOTHEKE
Körnerstrasse 19
71634 Ludwigsburg
Germany
www.linden-apotheke-
ludwigsburg.de
Design Ippolito Fleitz Group
www.ifgroup.org
Lighting Ansorg
Construction and carpentry
Bayerl & Demmelhuber,
Tögging
**Transparency lettering,
ceiling fresco** Ross & Partner,
Stuttgart

**LULU PETITE AT FERRY
BUILDING**
1 Ferry Building, SPC 19
San Francisco CA 94102
USA
www.lulupetite.com
Design: CCS Architecture
www.ccs-architecture.com
Graphics Michael Mabry
Design
www.michaelmabry.com
Contractor Eugene Hom, Plant
Construction, San Francisco,
CA

**MAGMA PRODUCT
STORE**
16 Earlham Street
London WC2H 9LN
UK
www.mymagma.com
Design Nikki Blustin, Blustin
Heath Design
www.blustinheathdesign.com
and Julie Blum
Inside Out Systems
37 A Chetwynd Road
London NW5 1BX
UK
**Structural engineering and
cardboard fabrication** SCA
Packaging
www.scapackaging,com

**MARNI ACCESSORIES
SHOP**
50 via della Spiga
20121 Milan
Italy
www.marni-international.com
Design Sybarite
www.sybarite-uk.com
Main contractor Modus srl,
Italy
Specialist supplier Soozar,
China
Project team Simon Mitchell,
Torquil McIntosh, Filippo
Ferraris, Nicola Hawkins, Tara
Robertson, Giuseppe Giordano

MARTINE SITBON
Seoul, Korea
(store now closed)
Designed by Cho Slade, who
have since divided into three
practices: Moongyu Choi, Ga.a
Architects
www.gaaarchitects.com
Mass Studies
www.massstudies.com
Slade Architecture
www.sladearch.com

MOBILE JOKER STORE
Spitalerhof 8
Hamburg
Germany
www.mobilejoker.de
Architecture project team
Susanne Buckler, J'orn Hadzik
– Spine Architects
www.spine-architects.com

MYKITA
Rosa-Luxemburg-Strasse 6
10178 Berlin
Germany
www.mykita.com
Design MYKITA
Lighting design Lars Grau
www.larsgrau.de

M.Y. LABEL
1F, 1-17-6
Ebisu-minami
Shibuya-ku, Tokyo
Japan
Design Masamichi Katayama,
Wonderwall
www.wonder-wall.com

PEYTON AND BYRNE
Heal's
196 Tottenham Court Road
London W1T 7LQ
UK
www.peytonandbyrne.com
Design FAT
www.
fashionarchitecturetaste.com
Mosaics Paul J Marks
www.pauljmarks.co.uk

PHILIPPE DUBUC
4451 Rue Saint-Denis
Montreal
Quebec H2J 2L2
Canada
Architecture Saucier +
Perrotte Architectes
www.saucierperrotte.com

A PIECE OF CAKE
Importanne Galleria
Iblerov Trg bb
Zagreb
Croatia
Design Ivana Franke and
Petar Mišković

SHU
St Lucy Street
Valletta
Malta
www.exitmalta.com
Design Chris Briffa, Bernard
Vella, Marcia Calleja – Chris
Briffa Architects
www.chrisbriffa.com
Woodwork Saw Ltd
Wrought ironwork MMCS Ltd
Lighting Brilliant
Textiles Camilleri Paris Mode

SIS. DELI + CAFÉ
Lapinlahdenkatu 3
Kamppi
Helsinki
Finland
www.SISdeli.fi
Design Muotohiomo
www.muotohiomo.com
Illustration Klaus Haapaniemi
www.klaush.com

SNEAKERS DELIGHT
Rua do Norte, 30–32
Bairro Alto
Lisbon
Portugal
www.sneakersdelight.pt
Design Igor Vidal Ferreira
Illustration Skwak
www.skwak.com

SUNAO KUWAHARA
B1F b6 Jingumae
6-28-6
Jingumae
Shibuya-ku
Tokyo
Japan
www.a-net.com
Design Steve Lidbury Design
(practice now dissolved)

TIMBUK2
506 Hayes Street
San Francisco, CA 94102
USA
www.timbuk2.com
Architecture William Duff
Architects
www.wdarch.com
Contractor Norcal
Management Services

UBIQ
1509 Walnut Street
Philadelphia, PA 19103
USA
www.UBIQlife.com
Design Rafael de Cárdenas,
Architecture at Large
www.architectureatlarge.com

UNION NY
176 Spring Street
New York, NY 10012
USA
www.unionyc.com
Design Harry Allen &
Associates
www.harryallendesign.com

WATX
Passeig de Gracia 42
08007 Barcelona
Spain
www.watxshop.com
Design Martí Guixé
www.guixe.com

WELLIE WAGON
New York, NY
USA
Fabrication and design
TEAMcreative
http://proteus.meccahosting.
com/~a0004183/
Client Tretorn
http://www.tretorn.com

THE WRONG STORE
was briefly in existence at
Galerie Frédéric Giroux
8 Rue Charlot
75003 Paris
http://www.fredericgiroux.
com
Design: Cyril Duval, Item Idem
www.itemidem.com

Page numbers in *italics* refer to picture captions

6 Jenny Nordquist
8 Courtesy of Alessi
9 Courtesy of Paul Smith
10 The Courtauld Institute of
   Art, London
11 left The Courtauld Institute
   of Art, London
11 right Kurt Forstner
12 top Aslak Raanes
   http://aslak.raanes.name/
12 bottom Courtesy of Kartell
13 top Masaya Yoshimura/
   Nacasa & Partners Inc
13 bottom Matthew
   Winterburn
14 left courtesy of the author
14 right Jorge Matreno
15 The Courtauld Institute of
   Art, London
16 Courtesy of the author
17 left Courtesy of Nuance-
   Watson (HK)
17 right courtesy of the
   author
18 Per Mosseby
19 Simon Roberts
20 Oliver Heissner
22–23 Todd Eberie
24 Dan Stevens
25 Carlo Draisci
26–31 Floto + Warner/MS
   Logan Ltd
32–37 Courtesy of Steve
   Lidbury Design
38–43 Oliver Heissner
44–49 Courtesy of
   Lipthay+Cohn+Contenla
50–53 Courtesy of Soldier
   Design
54–59 © Zooey Braun
   Photography
60–65 Courtesy of Ryuji
   Nakamura Architects
66 Ivan Sarenas
68–71 Kozo Takayama
72–77 diephotodesigner.de
78–81 Joshua McHugh
82–87 © Dennis Gilbert/VIEW
88–93 © Photography by
   Morley von Sternberg
94–99 Jean Longpré

100–105 Courtesy of Nigel
   Coates
106–111 Courtesy of EKO
112–117 Jungsik Moon
118–123 Jeremy Crowle
124–129 Pablo Orcajo
130–135 Daniel Stegemann/
   netzextrakt
136–141 Nienke Klunder
142–145 Ivan Sarenas
146–149 Courtesy of Le Labo
150–155 Kozo Takayama
156 Courtesy of MYKITA
158–161 Courtesy of Steve
   Lidbury Design
162–165 JD Peterson
   Photography
166–169 Sami Repo
170–175 James Finch
   (Magma)
176–181 Jorge Matreno
182–187 Inga Knölke/
   Imagecontainer
188–191 Cesar Rubio
   Photography
192–195 Courtesy of Sybarite
196–201 Courtesy of MYKITA
202–207 Courtesy of Marc
   Newson
208–213 Chris Briffa
   Architects
214–219 Bogdan Zupan
220–225 Courtesy of M-M
226–231 © Thierry Malthy
232–235 Martin Kunze,
   Hamburg
236–239 Kristina Lenard and
   Robert Les
240–243 Courtesy of FAT
244–247 Courtesy of Tretorn
248–249 Courtesy of Item
   Idem

AUTHOR ACKNOWLEDGEMENTS

Working on this book has been a pleasure, not least due to my editor Liz Faber at Laurence King and those designers and retailers who kindly took time to discuss the shops in this book. I would also like to thank Trish Lorenz, Clare Dowdy, Paul Ettedgui and Sarah Balmond for their support and/or suggestions.